Also by Rev. Jim Webb

Pathways to Inner Peace:
Lifesaving Processes for Healing Heart, Mind and Soul

The Keys to Enlightened Living:
Channeled Messages from the Masters

THE

SOUL

OF

PROSPERITY

Rev. Jim Webb

Table of Contents

6 MEDITATION: THE JOURNEY BEGINS WITHIN

Exercises

How to Read This Book

Imagine that you are planning a cross-country trip to multiple destinations. In *The Soul of Prosperity*, you:

> **Create your roadmap**—*Prosperity Worksheet*s that you refine by repeating them several times provide the directions that you follow to reach your chosen prosperity destinations. Initially, you choose three specific destinations. You can, of course, choose additional destinations but, in order to maintain focus, I recommend that you start with three. You can add more later. You might also want to use a notebook instead of, or in addition to, the worksheets.

> **Identify obstacles**—Much of the book is about the types of obstacles you might encounter along the way and helping you to identify specific obstacles that apply to you.

> **Identify tools**—Various tools (methods) throughout the book allow you to prepare yourself for departure, and to avoid mechanical failures, detours, and roadblocks along the way.

To get the most out of this book, I recommend that you read it in any of the following ways:

> **Straight through, then repeat**—Reading straight through will familiarize you with the content, and then you can return to the beginning, reacquaint yourself with any areas that you need to review, and begin doing the exercises in the order they are presented. This approach gives you the big picture, and can actually get you started on your

pathways to prosperity even before you complete the exercises.

Once through, doing the exercises as you go—Pausing to do, and even repeat, the exercises as you read the book for the first time is also a powerful way to address any issues that have kept you from enjoying the prosperity that is available to you. As you proceed, you will see yourself drawing nearer to the prosperity that awaits you. This is actually the approach that I intended for you to take when I wrote the book.

Focused approach—I have provided a detailed table of contents and a list of exercises so that, when you have completed the book and the exercises, you can conveniently revisit any part of the book and focus on information that you find particularly valuable on your journey to prosperity.

Whichever way you choose, you will notice that I sometimes repeat myself, sometimes expressing the same idea in a different way and using different examples. This is by design. I want to get inside your head, erase certain thoughts and images that have been obstacles that have kept you from attaining the prosperity that you seek, and replace these obstacles with new thoughts and images that will serve as guideposts along the pathways to your prosperity.

You will also notice that I provide you with a lot of information before and between the exercises. This, too, is by design. Think of the exercises as stopping points along the way. Just as when you are on any journey, I want your stopping points to have purpose, and not be off the route, in the wrong direction. I also want you to know why you are stopping, just as you stop during a trip to refuel, get snacks, fix a flat tire, or enjoy a scenic overlook.

If I have succeeded, you will find by the time you finish the book that not only have you begun to enjoy your prosperity, you will also have developed lifelong habits of prayer and meditation that will last long after you reach your destinations. I want your prosperity destinations to be not just places that you visit, but places where you live as your default, new way of being.

CHAPTER 1

WHAT IS PROSPERITY?

While it is widely believed that the *law of attraction* draws prosperity *to us*, it is equally true that we can use the same law of attraction to draw us *to our prosperity*. In other words, we can navigate our way to our prosperity as it finds us.

The Soul of Prosperity and the pathways that it offers are like a set of driving instructions that you can use to navigate your way to prosperity and, at the same time, draw prosperity to you.

The pathways to prosperity are quite simple. They combine ancient wisdom and common-sense practices with personal growth techniques such as meditation and creative visualization. Along the way on your journey to prosperity, you build a new, more fulfilling relationship with yourself, with others, and with the world around you. As a result, you experience peace within, and fulfillment in your outer world.

On this simple journey, you make simple choices. You can repeat these choices until you integrate them into the deepest levels of your thinking, actions, and reactions to your experiences. These choices bring new understandings that become an integral part of you, inspiring you to new actions as you move naturally forward on your journey of healing and transformation.

Actually, you have already begun this journey, but may not be aware of its purpose, or of the lessons available to you. You have been traveling by trial and error, as if you are driving along a dark, narrow road without lights, coming to dead ends, running into ditches and obstacles, traveling in circles, and experiencing upset and frustration before taking lessons and choosing a new route.

Without a map, or a clear vision of your destination or how to get there, the journey can seem tedious, pointless and unnecessarily difficult. Wouldn't it be great to move forward effortlessly and joyfully to wonderful destinations that you choose?

By following the pathways to prosperity, you can avoid much of the trial and error and create deep prosperity in every part of your life. This journey is your human process, and the pathways that you take to prosperity can be direct, simple and effortless when you know your purpose, your destination and the *rules of the road. The Soul of Prosperity (Pathways to your Good)* simplifies this journey, making it easier for you to move forward as smoothly as possible.

Prosperity is Like Pornography

To paraphrase Supreme Court Justice Stewart Potter when trying to define pornography (obscenity), "I shall no longer attempt to define it, but I know it when I see it."

Prosperity is like pornography in that we don't know what prosperity is, but we know it when we feel it. When we feel a sense of peace, fulfillment, faith, hope, and joy, we know we have reached a new level of prosperity.

Prosperity is Multidimensional

Our level of prosperity can change depending on how we see it. Like a beautiful, multifaceted diamond that sparkles and shines differently when we see it from different viewpoints, prosperity has many dimensions, and our perception of prosperity changes depending on how we look at it. We may already *be* prosperous based on our own inner standards of prosperity, but we may not *feel* prosperous because we believe that someone else's standards for prosperity will make us happy.

The Dimensions of Prosperity

Prosperity has at least six dimensions (areas). These dimensions are the possible destinations on your journey to prosperity.

- Relationship prosperity
- Family prosperity
- Occupational prosperity
- Financial prosperity
- Physical prosperity
- Spiritual prosperity

Relationship Prosperity

When we prosper in our relationships, we feel a sense of harmony with others. We experience less drama, friction and discomfort. The time that we spend with people is more of a joy than a burden, and time seems to stand still, because we feel a strong rapport.

For example, as a youth, I observed the long goodbyes that my mother and her best friend shared. They talked for hours, weaving seamlessly from just one more topic to the next. They tried to shorten their visits so they could attend to other things, but they kept starting a new thread of conversation. This would go on for hours, and as we finally were really leaving my mother would invariably say, "I don't know where the time went." As we left, she seemed like a new person. She was exhilarated, focused, and unburdened. She was at peace.

In my own relationships, I have a friend with whom the conversation weaves from subject to subject as the time passes

3

joyfully. Even after a long absence, when we get together it is as if we have just seen each other in the past week. Being with him is like putting on a pair of comfortable shoes that I had forgotten that I owned. This is relationship prosperity.

Family Prosperity

We know when we experience prosperity in our families because we find our family relationships to be supportive and uplifting, and we look forward to interacting with our family members. In other words, we have family prosperity when we are relating to our families in a functional way.

When we have family prosperity, we feel free to be who we are with our families, and we feel free to let our family members be who they are when they are around us. Family prosperity contains a minimal amount of judgment, competition, anxiety, discomfort or friction because there are no debts or regrets. We don't need our family members to be or act in a certain way for us to feel good about ourselves, and they don't need us to be or act in a certain way for them to feel validated.

This may seem like an impossible dream, but it is certainly possible by following the pathways to prosperity.

Occupational Prosperity

When we have occupational prosperity, we find occupational fulfillment and success, and we enjoy our work. We know that we are not experiencing occupational prosperity when we are bored or burned out. If we generally enjoy doing what we do so much that time seems to stand still and we would do it for free, then we know that we have reached a high level of occupational prosperity. Occupational prosperity often leads to financial prosperity.

Financial Prosperity

We know that we have financial prosperity when we have financial peace. Regardless of whether we are working with a $20,000 budget or a $2 million budget, we have financial prosperity when our physical and survival needs are fulfilled and our finances are a source of peace instead of worry. If we have a six-figure income accompanied by a seven-figure debt, we may actually experience less financial prosperity than someone who lives on significantly less. Our finances may then be a source of worry that affects every dimension of our prosperity, including our physical prosperity.

Physical Prosperity

Physical prosperity is more than physical health. It is a sense of well-being and physical comfort that brings us a sense of peace. Another dimension of physical prosperity is logistical ease. Those with hellish commutes rarely experience this degree of physical prosperity.

Often, we associate physical prosperity with a minimal amount of stress and its damaging side-effects, such as an increased risk of heart attacks, and strokes, and a reduced resistance to illness. Studies have shown that regular meditation reduces stress and its side effects. Meditation also increases our spiritual prosperity.

Spiritual Prosperity

We know that we have spiritual prosperity when we attain a sense of inner peace, the peace that passes all understanding, and we feel a connection with something larger than ourselves. When we feel spiritual prosperity, any challenges we face seem temporary, and we are well aware of what we can do to overcome these challenges.

We have spiritual prosperity when we have developed ways to navigate these challenges and to remember our connection to a Source of love and joy. We know that we are experiencing spiritual prosperity when we no longer have an ongoing sense of anxiety, fear, doubt or worry.

CHAPTER 2

WHY HAS PROSPERITY ELUDED US?

Often, we have let Wall Street, Hollywood, Madison Avenue, or a combination of the three, define our prosperity.

We have let Wall Street define our prosperity when we believe that prosperity is only available on the condition that we attain a certain level of monetary and material wealth.

We have let Hollywood define our prosperity when we believe that the images projected by Hollywood—which are illusions created by make-up, stringent preparation, planning, a cast of thousands and a budget of millions—depict a perfect lifestyle. In Hollywood, solutions to challenges are resolved neatly within an hour or two, and we assume that all the good guys will live happily ever after.

We have let Madison Avenue (the advertising world) further define our prosperity by believing that if we buy the products that they sell, we will have the fantasy life depicted by Hollywood and we will be worthy of love.

The problem with external definitions of prosperity is that they invite us to strive for unrealistic, non-existent illusions based on unattainable standards of perfection. These illusions guarantee constant dissatisfaction.

Note that when we defined the dimensions of prosperity, there were no absolutes that indicated when we were or were not experiencing prosperity. There were just general *feelings* of prosperity or the lack thereof. In other words, we can define prosperity any way we choose. The reason that we often do not experience prosperity is because we have let others define it for us, and we believe that we must attain their standards in order to prosper.

Why Prosperity Has Eluded Us

Prosperity has eluded us for any of three reasons:

We do not know that there is a set of principles and laws that create prosperity—When we understand that our inner awareness (our conscious and subconscious minds working in harmony) creates our prosperity, we have our first clue as to why prosperity has eluded some of us. We haven't realized that the true engine of prosperity is our own subconscious mind.

We do not know that we can use these principles and laws to create our prosperity—Prosperity may have eluded us because we haven't realized that it is available to us. We have been conditioned to believe that prosperity is something outside of us, beyond our control and unavailable to us.

We haven't integrated these laws into our personal life practices—We may not have been aware of many of the tools and techniques that can create prosperity. Even someone who may have been aware of these techniques may not have regularly applied them so they can integrate them into their lives.

We Let Others Define Our Prosperity

We have become very skilled at letting others define every aspect of our happiness. This happens very gradually as we respond to feedback that we receive from others and from the world. Each time we receive positive feedback, we repeat the actions that we have taken to elicit it. When we receive negative feedback, we avoid the behaviors that have drawn it to us because we subconsciously fear that we will not get what we need to survive. Unfortunately, this behavior pattern keeps us from being the person we want to be and forces us into being someone we are not.

To demonstrate this, a group of students in a large lecture hall decided to play a joke on a professor who had a habit of pacing the floor of the auditorium. Each time the professor moved to the right of the podium, the students became inattentive. They talked among themselves, rattled papers, and otherwise created commotion. When the professor moved to the left of the podium, the students became silent and stared in awe at the professor. By the end of the lecture, the students had driven the professor to the far-left corner of the room, where he cowered and shouted at the top of his lungs!

The professor was amazed to find himself withering in a far corner of the cavernous lecture hall, driven there by the feedback he received from his students. He was not conscious of his drift, but subconsciously he told himself, *If I react by moving to the left, the students will show me the respect and attention that I desire.* Subconsciously, the professor equated this respect and attention with the core human need for love. He then responded to the feedback he equated with love, and let himself be driven into a corner of the room.

We Let Our Environment Define Our Prosperity

Since birth, we have received feedback from the world in the same way the professor received it from his class. This feedback drives our behavior.

The feedback that we receive is *conditional feedback*. That is, if we meet certain conditions, we receive positive rewards: love, positive attention, and admiration. If we don't meet those conditions, we receive negative rewards: criticism, punishment, and shame-inducing responses.

I'm sure you can think of examples of how you have modified your behavior to please others. In most cases, these reactions have been subtle and innocuous. In other cases, our people-pleasing behaviors may have caused us to betray our true essence.

We Concoct Stories Based on This Feedback

When we are children, our parents and families truly hold the keys to our survival, because they provide us with our food, shelter and protection. When they withhold love and approval from us, we subconsciously fear that they will withhold the means for our survival, because love and approval are core needs. We subconsciously perceive that we are in mortal danger, and we respond to this danger by modifying our behavior according to their wishes. Our parents learned to control our behavior by withholding, or threatening to withhold love and approval when we behaved in ways that did not meet their standards.

Since everyone is trained from birth to understand this dynamic, others also use this dynamic to elicit the behavior they want from us. By giving positive feedback for desirable behavior, and either withholding positive feedback or giving negative feedback when we exhibit behavior they want to discourage, they manage our behavior, our perceptions of ourselves, and our sense of well-being. Just as the professor was forced into one corner of the room, we are forced into a way of thinking and behaving that may not reflect our true nature but, instead, reflects someone else's desires for us based on their world view, their fears, their desires, Subconsciously, we believe the stories that this feedback creates.

Our Stories Limit Our Prosperity

There are many ways that our stories can limit our prosperity. For example, a parent who feels inadequate because he or she didn't have the educational opportunities that are available to you may have stressed education to you. Their emphasis on education may have been so pronounced that their love for you may seem to be conditional based on your academic performance, regardless of your native abilities, aptitudes, or interests. You may have wanted to be a carpenter, but your parents wanted you to be a doctor. Their way of showing love for you was to push you, judge you, scold you, or shame you if you didn't meet their standard of perfection based on what they wanted for you. Your self-esteem may have suffered because you believed that your worth was dependent on meeting their criteria for perfection.

In another example, your parents or parental images may have an idea of which body type and physical characteristics are lovable. They may have grown up in an era where survival and self-worth were dependent on being loved by someone, and being loved by someone was dependent on having certain physical and social characteristics. Out of love, they may have wanted to mold you into a person who has such characteristics so you would survive and have the love that they desired for you. Consciously or subconsciously, they shamed you into believing that you had to look a certain way and be of a certain weight in order to get the love that they wanted you to have.

This conditional love may have had the short-term effect of controlling your behavior, but it also had a pernicious long-term effect of planting stories in your mind that compromised your self-worth and your ability to experience prosperity. The effect that these stories have had is quite evident in many of the people I have counseled.

One such client is Judy, the middle child in her family, who felt she was not seen, heard or valued because she didn't receive the attention that the oldest child received, and felt she was ignored when her younger sibling was born. Judy is left-handed and always felt different and flawed. In her heart, she has collected a whole catalog of slights. Anytime something unpleasant happens to her, she believes that it is because she is a left-handed middle child, because this is the *story* that she tells herself.

Another client, Joe, has received constant criticism from perfectionist parents who want him to be all that he can be. This criticism implies that he is not good enough just as he is. In his heart, he has told himself the story that he is not good enough, and he can't finish projects for fear of withering criticism. The story that he subconsciously tells himself is that If he doesn't finish, he won't get criticized. This has had negative effects on his life and career. He is disappointed by a lack of fulfillment, and his heart is breaking.

A third client, Chris, received attention from her parents when she was sick, and she perceived this attention as love. In her heart, Chris associates being ill with receiving love, so she subconsciously opens herself to being sick in order to get the love that she needs to survive, but she doesn't understand why she can't seem to get well.

In these examples, my clients have told themselves stories about their *left-handedness*, their *not-good-enoughness* and their *sickness*. We have all told ourselves similar stories. These stories diminish us and keep us from fulfilling the potential that lies within each of us. It is as if the part of ourselves that we have rejected is living in the basement of our minds, where it is held hostage and cannot escape. What holds this part of us back are the stories that we tell ourselves or that we have been told by others. These stories are as fictional as a fairy tale, but to us they are very real in the same way that an elephant, tethered since infancy to a small stake in the ground, continues into adulthood to believe it cannot move. The adult elephant has the strength to simply walk away, but the childhood memory of being tethered to the stake convinces the elephant that it cannot escape.

CHAPTER 3

HOW DOES PROSPERITY BEGIN?

Prosperity begins when we define it on our own terms, based on our own standards, and not according to someone else's standards. Prosperity occurs naturally as we heal and reshape our inner awareness, with our conscious and subconscious minds working in harmony. We can change our inner awareness by integrating the laws of prosperity into our lives. We discuss these laws in more detail in the next chapter but, first, let's pause to consider why we care about these laws.

Our Grand Vision

Despite all of our doubts and fears, somewhere deep within we hold the grandest vision of ourselves. You know in your heart that this is true. Still, we are often unable to achieve this grand vision due to the stories we have told ourselves or that we have been told by others. When we are able to make and sustain our connection with this grand vision of ourselves, we can integrate it deeply into our everyday experience. Constant exposure to this grand vision, and constant connection to the emotions and feelings that this vision creates, make it happen. Our connection to the Source of unconditional love nurtures this vision because it negates the pernicious effects of conditional love and neutralizes the destructive stories we have told ourselves that keep us from attaining prosperity.

What stories have you been told about prosperity? What left-handedness, not-good-enough-ness or sickness stories do you tell yourself? Whatever they are, these stories are based on your experiences of conditional love. They have blinded you to the prosperity that is available to you and to everyone.

Each day, you receive feedback from the world and you let the world define prosperity for you. Deep in your heart, you may feel perfectly prosperous as a single person, but you may have received constant feedback from a world that tells you that you can only be prosperous if you have a spouse, 1.2 children, and a house in the suburbs with a white picket fence. When you listen to the world's definition of prosperity instead of to your own internal truth, you may trade your grand vision of yourself, your true inner prosperity, for a definition of prosperity that in fact leaves you feeling unfulfilled. When it does, remember:

To attain prosperity, define it on your own terms.

How Do You Define Your Own Prosperity?

To define your own prosperity:

Learn your own internal prosperity standards.

Become comfortable with *your* standards so you do not sacrifice them for someone else's. This requires an *inner awareness*, which is a deep, lasting understanding of *what makes you tick*.

Becoming Aware of Your Consciousness

Your *consciousness* includes both your conscious and your subconscious mind. You begin defining your own prosperity as you become more aware of both. Your consciousness is the grand combination of your thoughts, feelings, experiences, and reactions to your environment. Some you remember (conscious) and some you don't (subconscious).

Your conscious and subconscious minds share an internal database where you record everything. When something happens, you do a record check *with both minds* into your database and draw conclusions based on past experiences. Then you react to the event in order to either avoid pain or to pursue joy.

For example, if you smell a familiar perfume, the invisible molecules of that perfume emanate from the person wearing the perfume and touch the sensitive olfactory nerves in your nose. These nerves vibrate in response to the stimuli and create an electromagnetic impulse that is carried through the central nervous system to the brain. The brain matches the electromagnetic impulse to the stimuli that it has stored in the same way that a Google search matches information queries against a database. Your mind's Google goes to the *perfume* category, where you may have a number of different fragrances stored away, so you match the smell with the appropriate perfume and you have the thought, *She's wearing Chanel No. 5.*

Subconsciously, when this match is made, all the associations for it come up. You may associate the fragrance with a person with whom you have had an extremely positive experience, and subconsciously you want to re-create the experience. Or, you may associate the fragrance with someone with whom you have had a negative experience, and subconsciously you want to avoid creating another negative experience. Consciously, you may simply be aware of the fragrance of Chanel No. 5. Subconsciously, this experience may trigger a wide range of thoughts, experiences, emotions and associations.

Often, you are not really aware of all that makes you tick. Everybody wants to be prosperous, healthy, wealthy, wise, fulfilled and happy. So, why can't you just wiggle your nose like Samantha Stephens, the witch in the popular 1960's and early

1970's television series *Bewitched*, and magically attain prosperity? You can't because your subconscious mind often rejects the same prosperity your conscious mind says that you want. Your subconscious mind is at war with your conscious mind, and often overrules what you consciously desire.

In the perfume example, your desire to avoid another negative experience with someone wearing Chanel No. 5 may outweigh your desire to create a positive experience, even though you think you want to create a positive experience. For example, you may consciously want to create a loving relationship, but you associate a loving relationship with pain, abandonment, betrayal and struggle, none of which you want.

The creative force that creates your outer world is a dynamic combination of your conscious mind and your subconscious mind. Your subconscious mind may actually sabotage your conscious desire, so it is important for you to understand your subconscious mind and get it in harmony with your conscious desires.

Your Consciousness Is Like an Iceberg.

Twenty percent of an iceberg is above the surface of the ocean; eighty percent is beneath the surface. The part of the iceberg that sank the Titanic is the part that was beneath the surface, the lower eighty percent. Such is the case with your consciousness. Your subconscious mind lies beneath the surface of your conscious mind and sinks your desires.

For example, several years ago, a friend and I went together to buy supplies for a brunch we were hosting. He constantly complained that New Yorkers were so rude—especially clerks, who were always particularly nasty. He complained so much about how he often got into arguments with them that I could almost see what was coming. After placing the brunch items on the conveyor belt, my friend placed the Sunday paper on the counter out of sight to the clerk. When the clerk finished ringing up everything and asked for the money, my friend said, "You forgot the newspaper." The clerk had to void the transaction and wasn't sure how to do it. As she fumbled about, my friend became increasingly angry and impatient and demanded that the clerk ring up the newspaper separately, but the clerk had already begun the voiding process and insisted on doing it her way. Tensions mounted, tempers rose and a nasty argument followed, complete with name-calling, and the store manager got involved. As we left, my friend said, "See, I told you these clerks are nasty. They're always getting into fights with me," and, "You can't get good help." My friend didn't realize that he subconsciously created that situation. By placing the newspaper out of the clerk's field of vision, he created a self-fulfilling prophecy.

Because of his inner beliefs, my friend created a situation that diminished his prosperity in the moment. It was a powerful reminder that prosperity begins within. On our journey through the pathways to prosperity, we will discover how to find inner prosperity so our inner prosperity is reflected in our outer world.

CHAPTER 4

PROSPERITY LAWS: THE RULES OF THE ROAD

Prosperity laws are the driving directions that help you on your pathways to prosperity. Physical laws such as the law of gravity and the law of magnetism help us to navigate the earth more effortlessly because they show us how to navigate without pain. If we violate the law of gravity by jumping out of a third-story window, we are likely to get hurt. As long as we are aware of this law and abide by it, we can avoid serious injury.

Driving laws help us navigate the highway system with a reduced risk of pain and suffering. When we violate these laws, by running a red light, for example, at best we get a traffic citation, and at worst we cause ourselves or others bodily harm or even death.

These laws are real. Even though we can't see them, we see their effects every day. Prosperity laws are just as real. When we abide by the laws of prosperity, we are more likely to achieve and retain the prosperity that we desire. When we violate these laws, we are less likely to achieve the prosperity that we desire.

What is the Law of Vibration?

The spiritual *law of vibration* is based on the idea that everything is energy, made up of proton, neutron and electron particles. These particles orbit each other at a vibratory rate that can be faster (less dense, expanded) or slower (contracted) depending on circumstances. When we are depressed, fearful or angry, our energy is often slower (contracted), which is one reason that we tense up due to stress. When we are excited, joyful or at peace, our vibratory rate is expanded, and we become more relaxed. We can perceive and express more joy, and we have a sense of well-being.

For example, if you have an inherent fear of shopping that affects your vibration, you are more likely to become irritated and perhaps to confront others, as described further in, *What is the Law of Inner Cause and Outer Effect?*

What is the Law of Inner Cause and Outer Effect?

The spiritual law of inner cause and outer effect says that our subconscious attracts its reflection in our environment. Our subconscious holds the experiences generated and the energy (vibration) and beliefs that we carry based on those experiences.

To continue the example from the law of vibration, you might enter a store expecting to be treated a certain way by salespeople because you were born poor and looked down upon by others.

What is the Law of Attraction?

The law of attraction is a manifestation of the law of inner cause and outer effect.

The law of inner cause and outer effect says that, like a magnet, we are *capable* of attracting (outer effect) what exists in our subconscious mind (inner cause). The law of attraction is a physical demonstration of this capability. For example, you might actually attract an unpleasant encounter with a salesperson when you are angry or fearful and enter a store expecting to be treated a certain way by salespeople because you were born poor and looked down upon by others.

We can see the law of inner cause and outer effect in action when noting that, to gain approval, a child might perform up or down to our expectations. The child has learned that in order to gain the approval that it equates with the love, support and nurturing that it needs to survive, it must meet the expectations of its authority figure, and the child reacts in ways to meet those expectations. In essence, the child creates the desired outcome in order to get what it needs to survive. This child then tells itself the story of what it needs to do, how it needs to behave, and what it needs to accomplish in order to survive, and this story becomes a part of the child's consciousness. For example, a young girl may play with her hair or a young boy may offer a cute boyish grin if these actions repeatedly get them the approval they desire.

Psychologists call this phenomenon *conditioning*. Sociologists call it *socialization*. Laymen call it developing a habit. Others call this manifestation of the law of inner cause and outer effect, the law of attraction.

Quantum physicists have discovered that we build neural pathways as our consciousness develops. These neural pathways are the connections between our senses and our brains. They are formed when we associate a stimulus (such as an experience) with an emotional reaction (such as an association or memory when we smell a certain perfume). In the perfume example, the neural pathway is the route that the electromagnetic impulse travels from the olfactory nerves through the central nervous system to the brain. The emotional reaction to the smell is based on memories, and the expectation that the situations that are remembered will be repeated.

As the same information repeatedly travels on these neural pathways, our reactions to these stimuli become *hard-wired* patterns of behavior in the same way that if we repeatedly trample on our lawn to take a shortcut, we wear a path in the lawn. This hard wiring creates the expectation that we will continually repeat our experiences. When we repeat the experiences, the emotions that we feel produce chemical reactions (the secretion of hormones, enzymes, neuro-peptides, etc.) that affect and eventually change the cells in our bodies. That is, the cells in our bodies become accustomed to receiving the charge that these emotions generate and, as a result, the cells actually change. The burgeoning science of epigenetics studies these changes and how they can be passed down to future generations.

In other words, we tell the story to every cell in our bodies and this story becomes our norm. Our story becomes what we expect. Just as children learn to perform up or down to expectations, we subconsciously become dependent on this story. This story becomes our truth, and we have an investment in fulfilling our expectations by repeating this story, because repeating it gives us a sense of security.

This false sense of security is why we become enmeshed in destructive patterns such as damaging relationships, unfulfilling occupational pursuits, and unhealthy dietary and lifestyle choices. Even though we know we are engaging in destructive behavior, we believe that we need the experience in order to function and to live.

This is also why lab rats that become addicted to substances will ingest those substances until they die. A neural pathway in their brains has been formed, and the habit of the substance has become their new reality. The story that they must have the substance to survive has become their truth. They will then ingest the substance until they die because, ironically, they believe they must have the substance to live. By that same token, we become addicted to the fulfillment of the stories we have told ourselves, even if these stories are not true or are no longer necessary for our survival. This addiction gives rise to self-fulfilling expectations that may actually sabotage the prosperity we desire.

In keeping with the law of attraction, we attract and react to experiences that reflect our expectations instead of reacting to any of the many other experiences happening around us. According to scientists, the brain processes 400 billion pieces of information per second, but we're only aware of 2,000 pieces of information. We become aware of the crucial information we need in the moment and filter out the rest. Our brain operates this way even though we don't perceive its depth or complexity.

Our brain continuously commands our body to breathe, yet we rarely think about breathing. We don't perceive this continuous command and response. We filter out information that doesn't support the story that we have told ourselves just as we filter out information that we cannot use at the moment.

For example, Madonna released a song called *American Pie*, which was a re-make of an old song from the '70s. The first time I heard Madonna sing the song, I started singing the lyrics even though I had never consciously memorized them. The lyrics had been buried in my subconscious mind for over 30 years although I didn't realize that they were there. Our expectations are also often buried in our subconscious mind in the same way that song lyrics are buried there. When we perceive and react to the experiences that reflect our expectations, we set up a dynamic where our subconscious expectations are met.

In the perfume example, we may have smelled hundreds of fragrances, seen thousands of visual images, and filtered out billions of pieces of information in the same moment that we smelled the perfume.

The perfume also had a strong subconscious emotional charge that we reacted to because it reflected our story. To repeat, this type of manifestation of the law of inner cause and outer effect is caused by the law of attraction. When we understand how the law of attraction works, we can then modify our behavior patterns, create a new story, and attract circumstances that reflect our new story.

To attract prosperity, we adopt a prosperity consciousness in all the dimensions of prosperity. For example:

- To attract love, adopt a loving consciousness.
- To experience peace, cultivate a peaceful consciousness.
- To attract success, adopt a success consciousness.

We adopt a new consciousness by examining both our conscious and subconscious expectations. We tell ourselves a new story and, in the same way that we have been conditioned to the old story, we begin to live our lives according to our new story.

The Paradox of Perfection Limits Us

Our power of creation and attraction is an inherent part of us. However, many of the experiences that we have attracted and been attracted to are reflections of a damaging world view that we have been taught due to the paradox of perfection, which says, *I am imperfect, and therefore I don't deserve my good*. This paradox of perfection has been ingrained in our subconscious minds, causing us to judge ourselves negatively and to feel unworthy of our good. As a result, our subconscious mind has often overruled our conscious desire for prosperity. For this reason, we have been unable to gravitate toward or attract experiences that are fully loving in our outer world.

What is the Law of Innocence?

The law of innocence is based on the idea that as beloved children of God, we are born innocent and deserving of every benefit and blessing of God's grace. This is counter to one of the most pervasive stories we tell ourselves, which is that we do not deserve all the manifestations of prosperity. This story is particularly damaging because we are usually not aware that we are telling it to ourselves.

This story is based on the illusion of guilt. We will teach ourselves of our innocence and that we deserve prosperity. In the next chapter, we will describe the futility of the illusion of guilt so we can more fully appreciate the law of innocence.

The Power of Self-Appreciation

To better understand the law of innocence, we will learn to appreciate our uniqueness. When we begin to appreciate our uniqueness, we can use the power of self-appreciation to fuel our prosperity. When we are ready to appreciate our uniqueness and its purpose, we are no longer willing to consciously or subconsciously withhold our prosperity from ourselves. However, it is often difficult to see the purpose of any experience when we are in the middle of the experience. Instead, we dread the experience, judge it to be undesirable and miss the ultimate lesson. Only much later does the true benefit or lesson of the experience come to us.

For example, getting fired or laid off often creates dread or anxiety in our society based on the way we have learned to associate employment with worth, acceptance and lovability. However, there are literally millions of stories of successful people whose journey to success began with termination, usually from jobs where they were miserable anyway. Only from the pinnacle of their success can they see that in the *bigger picture* their short-term adversity was the catalyst for their ultimate success, and without the momentary adversity their success may not have come.

We have developed in a culture that rewards conformity and punishes uniqueness based on the paradox of perfection, which says that there is one standard of perfection and all else is flawed. As a result, we often discount the unique qualities that comprise the unique purpose of our individual lives. We learn to denigrate our greatest gifts, turning them into sources of shame and punishment. We subconsciously withhold from ourselves in the erroneous belief that our greatest gifts are the source of our deepest shame. Then we are forced to live in an unfulfilling corner of our world in the same way that the professor was forced into a corner of his vast lecture hall. We learn to reject our uniqueness and the unique plan for our lives.

Our Grand Vision in the Grand Plan of the Universe

Just as there is a grand vision deep within us, as described earlier, that we can integrate into our daily lives by connecting to it, there is also a grand purpose for all our lives, and there is value in the unique purpose that we all play in the grand plan for the universe. We may not see the grand plan for the universe from our perspective but, at times, we get glimpses of it in instances of synchronicity or coincidences.

When we align with this grand plan, and our unique path within this plan, we can live our lives with more joy and fulfillment. We align with this grand plan by working with the laws of prosperity. When we align with this plan, we see the universe as an ultimately benevolent force into which we can all be connected.

Imagine that this grand plan is like a wonderful tapestry that consists of multiple threads made of many colors, fabrics and consistencies. All the threads in the tapestry have equal value and contribute equally to its multi-dimensional beauty. If one thread is pulled from the tapestry, the whole tapestry falls apart.

When we choose to see the universe as such a wonderful tapestry, and when we choose to relish our uniqueness as a part of this tapestry, we can move into a deeper level of self-acceptance. This is the lesson whimsically taught by the story of Rudolf the Red-Nosed Reindeer, who was teased, labeled a misfit, and banished to the Island of Misfit Toys until his unique gift found its place in the grand plan.

We can begin to accept ourselves by noticing, without self-judgment, those unique qualities and experiences that make us ourselves. By delving into our subconscious minds, we can remember those unique qualities that we have forgotten in our haste to conform. By performing this inventory, and looking at our uniqueness without self-judgment, we begin to realize that we have assumed our guilt due to the paradox of perfection, and we can begin to embrace the truth of our innocence.

What is the Power of Expectation?

We know that children perform up or down to our expectations. They want to please us, and they believe that if they meet our expectations, they will please us and we will give them what they need to survive.

Charles Fillmore, one of the fathers of the New Thought movement, said that the universe is impersonal; it simply responds impersonally to our thoughts. Like a child, the universe responds as a reflection of our expectations. If you raise the level of your expectations, you raise the level of your experience.

To illustrate the power of expectation, think about a man who plays the lottery. He affirms over and over that he will win the lottery. He visualizes himself winning the lottery. He prays that he will win the lottery. However, every day when he checks his numbers and finds out that he didn't hit the numbers, he says, *I knew I wasn't going to win.*

Often, your real expectations are buried in your subconscious mind, which is why the inner work of prosperity is so crucial. As you repeatedly work through the layers of your consciousness to create your prosperity, it is important for you to understand the power of expectation. As you move forward on your inner journey, you can ask yourself, *What do I expect?*

Change your outlook to change your outcome.

What is the Power of Anticipation?

You can also make conscious use of the *power of anticipation*, which is the power to actually create something in advance of its physical appearance. You can increase your vibratory rate to meet the vibratory rate of your desire. In a sense, you take a shamanic journey to a different level of vibration (the plane of creativity) where your desire already exists in thought form, and you drag it down to you in the same way that you might point, click and drag with your computer mouse.

Once, I had company in the spring. It was too early to turn on the air conditioning, so I thought I would just turn on the attic fan, which was suspended over joists in my attic in such a way that to start it I had to climb into the attic and lean precariously over an area that had no support other than the drywall ceiling above the laundry room. I announced that I was going to turn on the attic fan and said jokingly, "Now watch me fall through the ceiling." Within moments, as I straddled the joists, my company heard a crash and rushed into the laundry room just in time to see my legs coming through the ceiling as I fell onto my washer and dryer.

Ensure that what you anticipate is what you really want.
What do you anticipate?

Are Anticipation and Expectation Denial?

No, you are not denying what you see before you. You are simply acknowledging that what you see before you is a product of your past consciousness, and now that you are developing a new consciousness, you anticipate a new outcome. You are flooding your mind, body and soul with a new truth, and this new truth and what it creates replace the old expectations, which were based on past experiences.

The Truth of Our Innocence

When we are ready to accept ourselves just as we are, we are ready to release the guilt created by the paradox of perfection. Then we can begin to undo the conditioning that blocks us from our prosperity. When we heal the conscious and subconscious guilt that creates pain and suffering, we can accept our innocence.

At first, a child is innocent. A child is filled with wonder, optimism, incurable curiosity and a zest for life and its experiences. A child touches everything, explores everything, examines everything and accepts everything.

As adults, it is our responsibility to keep the child safe. In our zeal to do so, we teach the child limits, boundaries, and fear. We do so by using conditional love as a tool of manipulation. We give approval based on certain conditions, and withhold approval or punish the child if those conditions are not met. The child is helpless and fully dependent on others for life during its formative years as it learns to seek approval and avoid punishment. The child equates approval with love and learns to fear that if it does not have approval, it will not get what it needs to survive. This shifts the child's motivations away from seeking joy toward avoiding pain. This is how as children we lose awareness of our innocence.

Later in life, we may have fleeting experiences of our innocence in the form of *beginner's luck*. We may momentarily forget others' limited expectations of us and let our *super-selves* shine through. Our brain, in its purest and most undistorted form, is a highly efficient super computer. Before it is contaminated with the limited expectations of others, it can calculate the mass of a basketball, the distance to the hoop, our muscular capacity, and the body movements necessary to sink the perfect basket into the hoop. But when we do, our peers react with shock and surprise and we subconsciously receive the signal that we are not supposed to be able to sink the perfect basket. We tell ourselves the story that in order to have the approval of others, we must modify our behavior to meet their expectations. Our beginner's luck fades because we learn that we are not supposed to experience the magic of the pure mind. We learn that we are not innocent and perfect just as we are, and we subconsciously feel that we don't deserve our good.

In order to create our good, we maintain our innocence and worthiness. Several years ago, a study was conducted of wealthy people. These people had earned their wealth in different ways. Some had inherited wealth, some had married wealth, some had been involved in organized crime and literally stole their wealth, and some had earned their wealth. These people were all quite different, but the one thing that they had in common was the belief that they *deserved* their wealth. This *sense of worthiness* is the mindset that we all attain if we want to live with purpose and passion and have a lasting experience with any type of prosperity such as financial security, good relationships, and a sense of peace.

The Law of Love

When we maintain our innocence and our perfection, we maintain a state of balance and peace. We can arrive at this state of peace though meditation and self-appreciation. This builds the healthy self-esteem that is essential for prosperity.

Often called self-love, *the law of love* has been maligned as narcissistic self-absorption that makes us obnoxious and inconsiderate. This characterization describes a distortion of self-love, when an extremely unbalanced regard for oneself disregards others, or the situation at hand. This extreme distortion is actually an overcompensation for a lack of self-love. True self-love is a balanced, loving approach to yourself and others that empowers both you and others to reach your full

31

potential. In order to eliminate the enemies of self-love, we neutralize them.

Self-Love Is the Key to Prosperity

To understand the law of love more fully, let us see how the laws of prosperity work together, culminating in the law of love as the key to prosperity.

Although we are typically unaware of our subconscious mind, in keeping with the law of vibration, our subconscious mind is an amalgamation of our experiences, observations and beliefs.

In keeping with the law of inner cause and outer effect, we make up stories as a result of these experiences, observations and beliefs, and these stories create a world view that is often unpleasant, despite our desire for prosperity.

In keeping with the law of attraction, we are attracted to the subconscious world view that our stories have created, and this world view is attracted to us.

Self-Love Overcomes the Paradox of Perfection

When we become aware of the stories that the subconscious mind creates, we can release the unrealistic standards of perfection dictated by the paradox of perfection, and the subconscious desire to withhold our good from ourselves. Then we are able to contact an inner and outer sense of unconditional love.

As we become more aware of the consciousness of love, and actively place ourselves in an internal state of awareness of loving energy, we experience this unconditional love from within. We can become aware of the subconscious enemies to our prosperity and transform our subconscious mind so it is in alignment with our conscious desires. As we bring these warring factions into alignment, we can more powerfully move toward our desires instead of subconsciously creating unintended experiences. Instead of creating the conflict and self-defeating patterns that are the result of the conflicting parts of our subconscious, we can create what we intend to create. With the power of love, we experience a wider realm of prosperity.

Prosperity is simply an inner and outer experience of loving circumstances that enable us to feel loved, lovable and loving.

Developing a balanced sense of self-love is the essential key to prosperity. We develop self-love by stripping away subconscious guilt, judgment and aspects of the perfection paradox, so we can consciously create our good.

Self-love is the key to prosperity.

CHAPTER 5

ROADBLOCKS TO PROSPERITY

As you undertake your journey to prosperity, it is important to understand your emotions. Although you may experience a whole range of emotions, it might be easier to see the array of emotions in one of two categories:

- **Emotions that reflect love** show us where we are vibrating with the unconditional love of God. Examples are the joyous anticipation that a child has before Christmas, or that we have prior to a big event: joy, peace, exhilaration and, of course, love itself.

- **Emotions that reflect fear** show us where we are not aligned with the unconditional love of God. Examples of fear are:

   o **Anger**—which is fear turned outward.

   o **Rage**—which is an expression of anger.

   o **Depression**—which is anger turned inward.

   o **Procrastination**—which is immobility due to fear.

Fear has many faces. They include hatred, hubris, divisiveness, defensiveness, paranoia, exploitation, dishonesty, and denial.

Fear is the absence of love, or an unawareness of its presence.

Identifying Your Emotions

Your emotions are *road signs* that can point you toward your prosperity, or cause you to veer away from it. At first, you may find it difficult to identify the root cause for your emotional state. You can do this by continually asking yourself why you feel a certain way. For example, when asking why being stuck in traffic makes you angry and anxious, you might eventually come to the root cause, which is your erroneous belief that the universe does not support you. You may also have a fear that you will be punished for being late, and that something such as a paycheck that you need for your survival might be withheld from you.

When things that you can't control happen, your sense of self-worth is threatened. In this situation, you may also feel threatened because the fear of being late makes you less than perfect, and fills you with a sense of shame. You may subconsciously tie your sense of self-worth to your ability to get to your destination on time.

Surviving a Self-Quake

I call any event that threatens your sense of self-worth a *self-quake* because it feels like the event will rock your world. A self-quake is the most common event that triggers an emotional flare-up.

Subconsciously, you may derive some portion of your self-worth from the way others see you, the way your spouse treats you, or from the actions of others. You cannot control any of these things, because all individuals have free will. When your sense of self-worth is dependent on the views or actions of others, you have an investment in their views or actions. A job assignment or any other event that you are responsible for is just an example of a time when your investment in the way that others see you is at risk. You may have a self-quake anytime something outside of yourself (outside of your connection with God) that you need to survive is at risk and triggers an emotional flare-up.

When you are in a private place where you cannot be overheard, you may release your emotions in any way that you find appropriate. You can state them, scream them, or moan them. By releasing your emotions, you make room for a new energy. As you invite this powerful energy into your subconscious, it replaces your emotions with a feeling of peace and security. This is the peace that passes all understanding. When you vibrate in this peace, you can only create reflections of it.

An innocuous situation may trigger a deep, primal fear of pain, suffering and death. These strong emotions are what cause self-quakes. In the example of being stuck in traffic, we see how cases of road rage may occur. Continually ask:

Why do I feel threatened?

You will eventually get to the root cause that created your self-quake. Subsequent prayer and meditation will outline the root cause of your emotional state.

Conquering Your Fears

As you recognize all your emotions as either love or fear, you can use the following wisdom to help you conquer your fears:

The process of eliminating fear begins with your mind.

First, know that there is a power, an energy and a great love that supports, sustains, protects and nurtures you. You may believe this energy is outside of you. As you experience this energy through prayer and meditation, the channel between you and this energy that you believe is outside of you becomes stronger. As you work with this energy more and more, you feel more physical manifestations of this energy working with you in every part of your life. This energy permeates deeper levels of your subconscious until it *becomes* your subconscious.

You can help this process through prayer and meditation by saying to the energy that surrounds you, which is the energy of God:

I am afraid. I am afraid of . . .

Then list your fears. As described above, when you are in a private place where you cannot be overheard, release your fears in any way that you find appropriate. State them, scream them, moan them, making room for a new energy, which replaces your fears with the peace that passes all understanding.

Do not deny your fears, for that will not release you from them.

You do not have to be ashamed of your fears. They are an illusion. They are just stories you are telling yourself based on a past that need not be. As you work to release them, they will be taken from you. You may repeat the following prayer:

Mother, Father God, please release me from these fears. The fears I experience do not give me peace, and Your will for me is to have peace. My will for me is to have peace. I align my will with Thy will. I give You permission to heal my mind, my body and my affairs. I give You permission to remove anything from my subconscious that would cause me fear. I ask that I know only Your peace. I cast my fears upon the water

*like crumbs of bread that get lost in the infinite ocean
of Your love. They are dissolved by the infinite power of
Your love, so I release my fears to You.*

Know that God is with you always. Know that God supports you. Know that God affirms you when others seem not to. Know of your goodness. Know of your graciousness. Know of your strength. Know of your brilliance. Know of your ability. You do not have to apologize to anyone. You do not have to feel less than anyone. You do not have to have fear, for the light of God within you is brilliant, and powerful, and creative, and resourceful, and strong and masterful. Know that this describes you.

As you move into this awareness of your lovability, you vibrate with more of the energy of unconditional loving acceptance. As you begin to experience the inner prosperity that can more effortlessly attract your outer prosperity, you can use the various techniques which are described later to consciously create what you desire because you have eliminated the subconscious creations that have caused you pain and suffering.

Guilt

Guilt is a pervasive, insidious emotion. We carry memories of our transgressions, and these subconscious feelings are like invisible weights that keep us from feeling the buoyancy of light that wants to manifest through us and raise our vibrations to lift us to a higher level of existence.

Guilt originated from our soul's perception that it is separate from God the Source. The soul mistakenly believes that because it emanated from God, and is an individualized expression of God, it is less than the Source, and therefore less

38

whole and less worthy of love. This misunderstanding has been compounded through eons of experiences that have been created as a result of this misunderstanding. The soul has forgotten that it was created as an individualized expression of God so the light of God could expand, create and thus be magnified. The soul only knows that it has moved away from the Source, and the soul feels the guilt of an errant child, and believes that simple acts of expression are transgressions.

I recently observed this guilt in action when visiting an elderly friend in a nursing home. My friend's roommate had a son who was well-to-do and powerful in life. Apparently, the son was also very busy because he visited his mother quite infrequently even though he lived in the area. Every time he visited, he raised holy hell about his mother's care. He terrified, bullied and harangued the staff like a typical playground bully. Through his bravado, it became clear to me and others that he was compensating for his feelings of guilt regarding his mother.

Guilt is useless.

Nothing changes the past. At any given point, each one of us is doing the best we can with what we know at the time. We have never really left the garden of God's love. We have remained in the beautiful flowers of that garden, and our task now is to remind ourselves of this truth. In this truth we are innocent, not guilty. In this truth we are perfect, not flawed. A large part of the healing process is remembering this truth, and thus remembering who we truly are.

We are individual expressions of God's love.

Guilt is the Enemy of The Law of Innocence.

A client and friend summed up guilt in the following way:

> *No matter where I am, I feel that there is somewhere else*
> *I should be. No matter what I'm doing, I feel that there is*
> *something else I should be doing. No matter what I'm*
> *experiencing, I feel that there is something else I should*
> *be feeling. Somehow, I always feel wrong and insecure.*

In essence, guilt is a deep, underlying feeling of insecurity that says that you are not enough just as you are. It gives rise to a deep, underlying concern that whatever the circumstances, things are not as they should be, and the good that you experience cannot be maintained. Guilt is the feeling that you are somehow defective, that you are left-handed in a right-handed world. This gives rise to the story that you don't deserve your prosperity, so you subconsciously reject the prosperity that would bring you joy.

I once read an interview with Janet Jackson that shows how we can subconsciously reject prosperity. Jackson told how an elementary teacher embarrassed her in front of the class. She subconsciously retained the shame of the incident for years, which contributed to a two-year bout of depression, and sometimes still rose up to torment her.

> *If you feel guilty, consciously or subconsciously, you are*
> *not alone.*

Guilt Is Based on the Paradox of Perfection.

As the pathways in our minds are formed, we learn to see the world in terms of how we can avoid pain. This begins early in our process of socialization as we learn to fear chastisement, punishment, ridicule, shame and embarrassment. In our formative years, authority figures use these fears to help mold our behavior into the model behavior that they believe will enable us to live happy, fulfilling lives based on how they have learned to see the world.

The human mind constructs a scenario based on this feedback. This scenario is the projection of the perfect circumstances that would avoid pain. We then believe that if our experience deviates from this scenario, we will experience pain. As a result, our minds have largely been trained to see the world in absolutes (good vs. evil, weak vs. strong, etc.) but the world is more complex, and shades of gray do exist (for example, laudable motives can often drive people to make regrettable choices).

This scenario of the perfect set of circumstances that would enable us to avoid pain exists only in our minds, and our struggle to avoid pain often becomes the cause of our pain. This paradox, *the paradox of perfection*, is created when the illusion of perfection becomes our driving goal. We will never achieve this perfect state because it is an illusion that exists only in our subconscious mind but, by relentlessly pursuing this phantom reality, we constantly beat ourselves up and cheat ourselves out of our prosperity. We create the story that tells us that we are not worthy of our prosperity. Based on this story of guilt, which is based on the paradox of perfection, we cause ourselves all manner of pain and suffering.

An example of the paradox of perfection, and how an illusion of perfection has been hard-wired into our experience, can be seen during adolescent development. It would be an understatement to say that some youths have inner conflicts regarding their sexuality. Much of this conflict comes from the paradox of perfection created in their adolescence when echoes of ancient ideas based on ignorance about sexuality taught that virginal behavior was perceived as perfection. This idea conflicts with the very real sexual feelings and urges caused by the biological changes (the secretion of hormones, enzymes, etc.) necessary for growth, procreation and human survival. For many, this conflict between the illusion of virginal perfection and biological reality became a scenario of good vs. evil, and many have judged themselves to be evil because they have yielded to the experiences that we now know to be natural outgrowths of the body's biological process of development. As a result of this conflict, many still feel sexual guilt and shame that blocks their prosperity.

This is just one example of how we subconsciously reject our prosperity. As a minister, counselor and healer, I often work with people when they are in their deepest pain. Initially, I was surprised to realize that much of their emotional trauma can be traced to inner conflicts due to religious beliefs. The dominant legal, social and cultural environment amplifies these beliefs and creates an idealized sense of what is perfect and, thus, acceptable in God's eyes. Many of my clients have felt that they were imperfect, and they suffered from a deep sense of unworthiness. As a result of this inner unworthiness, they unwittingly contribute to situations that cause them to feel inadequate in their outer worlds, and this deep sense of inadequacy eventually causes distress.

For example, through numerous television commercials and shows, a woman may internalize an idealized image of the perfect body type and lifestyle (for example, working mom vs. stay-at-home mom vs. whether to parent at all). She then judges herself negatively because she does not measure up to this standard of perfection, or she is in constant conflict because she makes choices that appear to be outside this standard of perfection.

This inner conflict is reflected in her outer world and, at best, may result in guilt, anxiety and self-sabotaging behavior. At worst, this conflict can have a pernicious effect on her mind, body and spirit, resulting in behavior patterns that are outwardly and inwardly self-destructive. Although she may appear outwardly confident, inwardly she may be filled with conflict, guilt and internalized shame that she cannot own, trace or accept. This conflict tears away at her self-esteem, diminishing her capacity to accept love, give love, and thrive with the love that truly feeds her soul. Due to social convention or a need to martyr herself for the sake of her children, she may be stuck in a relationship that does not feed her heart or soul. She may starve herself or overeat to heal a pain that she cannot name.

But when we see what we have created, individually and collectively—for example, war and discord based on centuries of hatred—we can choose peace and prosperity. In order to choose, we will begin to see the paradox of perfection as the illusion that it is, and give ourselves permission to live according to our unique purpose.

Sexual Guilt

Many of the ideas that have resulted in a consciousness of conflict and guilt have their root in our Judeo-Christian culture. For example, sexual shame and guilt are based on ancient teachings that became distorted when ancient Hebrew writings were translated from Aramaic to Greek, and they became distorted even further when the early church fathers' discomfort with sexuality and pleasure influenced the *interpretation* of these ancient teachings.

Then, as now, sexual arousal happened as naturally and effortlessly as breathing. Childbirth, menstruation and other physical mysteries also occurred, but early scholars could not explain or comprehend these mysteries because they did not have the benefit of the science of biology. As a result, physical mysteries, including sexuality, became enshrouded with fear.

Discomfort with sexuality was *not* a part of Hebrew tradition. The command "Be fruitful and multiply" (Genesis 1:28) was taken seriously. In Israel, a large family was a divine blessing, (Genesis 22:17; Psalm 127:3-4), sterility was a terrible curse (Genesis 30:1, 1 Samuel 1:6-8) and virginity was cause for mourning (Judges 11:37).

Anti-sexuality evolved in response to early Christianity's opposition to other pagan religions, where sensuality was celebrated through orgiastic rituals. For example, most people can recall the shame, guilt and confusion they felt about their emerging sexuality and masturbation. According to Christian theology, perfect people don't masturbate or have sexual feelings, but many adolescents masturbate at every available opportunity, causing sexual shame and guilt.

Fear of Hell

Subconsciously, we believe that if we deviate from the perfect norm, we will eventually suffer and *go to hell* and experience eternal suffering. However, the hell that looms largely in our subconscious mind is simply a metaphor that symbolizes an internal place of mental confusion.

The term *hell* is derived from the word Gehenna (the Greek contraction of Ben Hinnom) which was the name of a valley located southwest of ancient Jerusalem. In the Old Testament, the

Valley of Ben Hinnom is where children were burned alive during pagan rituals.

In the New Testament, Ben Hinnom (Gehenna) was a place where the city burned its rubbish and its plague victims in a never-ending fire. As a result, the idea of Gehenna Dnoora (which translates into *hellfire*) became a figure of speech associated with filth and corruption as well as the idea of deep mental confusion. However, the term Gehenna (or hell) was never used in the time of Christ. The interpretation of hell as a place of future punishment came later when Thomas Aquinas added his interpretation.

The fear of *burning in the everlasting fires of hell* has filled many generations with terror and guilt and kept us from living full and productive lives as we became hostage to the promise of future punishment. We have been manipulated by this fear as it has been embedded deep in our subconscious and influenced our actions and reactions, limiting our life experiences. As a result, we have learned to criticize ourselves, judge ourselves, and reject ourselves in a very deep way. Instead, we can learn to appreciate ourselves so we can allow ourselves to enjoy prosperity.

Anger

Anger is based on fear.

Anger is an outward expression of fear.

We feel that something vital for our survival is being withheld from us, so we feel threatened. We transfer this need into the current situation, and believe that our need will not be met. As a result, we react with anger.

Anger is so insidious because it masquerades just below the surface as a vaguely unpleasant resentment, or it is transferred to a situation that is not related to the root cause of the feeling. When we react in a way that is out of proportion to an event that triggers an outburst, it is because our anger, resentment, or frustration is misplaced.

I recently worked with a client who was extremely frustrated in his marriage. He acted out this frustration on the job instead of addressing it with his wife, resulting in his getting laid off. Interestingly enough, this change created an imbalance in his relationship that forced him to address his marriage. He eventually realized the core reasons for his frustrations and found productive ways to get what he felt he was missing in his marriage.

All that we need comes from within us, because we create it. As we remember our connection with God, we understand that God would not withhold anything from us. God is not a punitive being. God is a force that draws to us all that we create. As we come to this new understanding, we are able to release our anger, for we no longer fear God's retribution. We no longer fear that something we need for our survival will elude us. With this new understanding, we can express our anger, release it and transform it, and open ourselves to more of God's love and bounty.

Depression

Depression, or any form of self-rejection, is anger or fear turned inward.

Once again, we fear that something that is vital for our survival will be withheld from us and as a result we turn our anger inward toward ourselves. We often feel that we are not acceptable as we are and carry low-grade shame that rarely surfaces consciously.

We make ourselves vulnerable to the shame, self-hatred, self-rejection, and self-denial that slows our vibration.

These negative energies keep us from attracting our greatest good, and cause us pain. As we come to a new understanding of God's unconditional love for us, we no longer turn our anger inward and hurt, hate, and reject ourselves. As we feel God's complete and unconditional love coursing through us in prayer and meditation, it becomes inconceivable for us to hate ourselves or fear that God would withhold anything from us.

God is the life force as it is expressed through us.

So, we no longer need depression. We release it, and we raise our vibration to its natural state of buoyancy, expansion, and unconditional love.

Martyrdom

Martyrdom (also known as *The Martyr Syndrome*) is an enemy of self-love. Collectively, we subconsciously tell ourselves the story that to martyr oneself for others is a pathway to divinity, but martyring one's self is a pathway to pain and suffering.

It is easy to understand how this distortion originated. Early in human evolution, humans were pack animals who moved around in groups in order to survive. The belief that the survival of the group was more important than the survival of the individual became hard-wired into our subconscious mind and we believed that martyrdom and self-sacrifice were noble. Many spiritual texts also glorify the nobility of martyrdom, leading us to believe that we must emulate martyrs in order to be holy. Because we are depleted, this idea becomes imbalanced and we are unable to help ourselves or to help others.

47

Sometimes, the most loving thing we can do for a person is to empower them to be all they can be and reach their full potential. This keeps us from falling into the trap of martyrdom. Sometimes, an action that seems to be loving can actually be injurious to another person when it keeps that person from reaching their full potential. For example, in an airline emergency we are always instructed to place the air mask over our mouths before placing one over the child's mouth, because we are of no help to the child if we are rendered unconscious. This concept is called *giving from a full cup* and is the balanced way to give that does not create distorted relationships where we overcompensate due to guilt.

Imagine a mother who loves her child so much that she wants to shield it from all pain. Due to guilt, she subconsciously believes that she must earn the approval of others and will do so only if others think that she is a good mother. She believes that if her child experiences pain, she is not a good mother because her job is to shield her child from pain. She will do whatever it takes to match the fictitious image of what a good mother should be. She wants to keep her child from falling, hitting its chin on the coffee table or hurting itself as it learns to walk, so she carries the child around long past the time when the child should be able to walk. The child's bones and muscles don't strengthen, the legs become malformed and bowed. The child's social development may be delayed due to his inability to function independently, so he may fail to develop and thrive among his peer group, creating even more stress for the mother. The mother develops back problems as a result of carrying the child but believes that this martyrdom is ennobling. This is an example, albeit extreme, of how a misapplication of love can inhibit the growth of another and actually harm oneself and others.

We can each recall a situation where we have been guilted into an action or behavior due to someone else's expectations of us, or our expectations of ourselves, that create imbalanced relationships. Due to guilt, we have often provided conditional love masquerading as support of ourselves and others only to encounter dysfunctional outcomes such as criticism, withdrawal of love or approval, or rejection when our fictitious standards of perfection are not met.

The idea of martyrdom was further ingrained in us through stories in Greek Mythology, which often had a recurring theme of expulsion, struggle and redemption. Just as the biblical idea tells us that we were expelled from the Garden of Eden for our *original sin* and banished as prodigal children, a recurring theme in Greek mythology tells us that the Gods were banished from heaven and forced to come to earth to redeem themselves. Quite often, they had to undergo Herculean struggles, and overcome many obstacles such as the lure of the Sirens in order to prove their divinity. Ultimately, they proved their divinity and redeemed themselves as a result of their struggles.

This theme has also been repeated in modern stories such as *The Wizard of Oz*, where Dorothy Gale and her cohorts who, through their many trials and tribulations, proved themselves worthy of returning home to a place of peace and comfort by demonstrating that they had qualities that they believed they lacked, such as courage, intelligence, and a heart.

We have interpreted these stories through the prism of guilt, and we have focused on the struggle in order to atone for the sins and shortcomings that caused us to be banished from heaven. The true moral of these stories is not that we must struggle so our inherent divinity can come forward; the true moral is that we are inherently Gods ourselves. These trials can trigger us into remembering who we really are, but when we view them through the lens of our inherent wrongness, we mistakenly interpret them as proof that we need to atone for our sins.

Judgment

Judgment is an enemy of self-love.

Often, a blessing is disguised, so we judge it to be a curse. We then reject the teaching, healing or opportunity for growth that the situation presents. We also judge ourselves negatively for being part of a situation that does not fit what the paradox of perfection would dictate to be a perfect experience, and we miss the lesson, the healing or the opportunity for growth that the situation would otherwise give us. We then repeat the situation with a different script and cast because it has become a part of our story as we have re-created it.

I once went through a wrenching separation. I thought it was the end of my life, and I judged it to be the most horrible thing that could possibly have happened to me. I was devastated emotionally, financially, and spiritually.

What I thought at that time was the end of my life was actually the beginning of my new life. The spiritual lessons that I knew in my head made the long journey from my head to my heart. Lessons that I had grasped intellectually became a visceral part of me, because my wounded heart opened to a deep healing and let the physical and spiritual experience of these truths shift my awareness onto a path of deeper self-love. These lessons were all I had to hold onto and they actually saved my life, which I considered taking more than once during my period of despair.

Although I self-judged this separation to be imperfect because it wasn't the ideal, picture-perfect life that the perfection paradox would dictate, it was part of a perfect life-purpose designed to shift my focus into a new realm that ultimately would help me and many others. In human terms, it was far from perfect, but in spiritual terms it was absolutely perfect.

Much of our pain is caused when we resist the grand purpose for our lives which, as described earlier, we fail to see, miss the lesson and get stuck in our story. We want things to be different than they actually are. We can't accept the experience we are having because we compare it to the image dictated by the perfection paradox, and we judge the experience and ourselves. Our inability to accept ourselves or the situation puts us in emotional fight or flight and we are not open to the healing, teaching or opportunity for change that the experience would give to us.

I am reminded of an ancient Chinese proverb of *The Lost Horse*, which has many versions. Here is one version:

> *The prized horse of a wealthy Chinese man's son ran away and was captured by enemy barbarians. The son's friends tried to comfort him, but his father said, "Perhaps this is a blessing."*
>
> *Months later, the horse returned, accompanied by a handsome stallion. The son's friends congratulated him, but his father said, "Perhaps this is a disaster."*
>
> *One day the son was riding the stallion and he fell off and broke his leg. His friends tried to comfort him, but his father said, "Perhaps this is a blessing."*

*The enemy came heavily armed to retrieve the stallion
and many lives were lost, but the son's leg was broken
and he could not go into battle, so he was spared.*

Good fortune turns bad, and bad turns good.

What we learn from this story is that when we accept ourselves, we can accept our experiences and flow with them, learn from them and grow because of them. It is rarely helpful to judge our experiences, our paths or our past based on our very limited perspective. There is often a larger picture that helps us to make sense of the seemingly senseless. As we accept our experiences and our circumstances, we also release judgment of ourselves for having had these experiences. We can then accept ourselves just as we are and teach ourselves unconditional love. We can internalize this self-love at the deepest subconscious levels so we can create loving experiences in our outer world.

As discussed earlier, self-love is what we have been leading up to. Self-love is the key to attracting our prosperity. With this awareness, we will now continue on our journey to self-love.

CHAPTER 6

MEDITATION: THE JOURNEY BEGINS WITHIN

Meditation has been called *listening to God*. It can be used to uncover the subconscious thoughts that would otherwise sabotage our conscious desires. As we become more adept at meditation, we realize that, through this process, we open to a powerful creative force. We become accustomed to the stillness of meditation, and the subtle energy that flows through us when we meditate.

The creative force we open to can take many forms. It can take the form of a sense of well-being that makes us feel safe and protected. It can take the form of a union with an energy that makes us feel as if we're connected to something bigger than our human experience, as if we are connected to everyone and everything. This powerful, spiritual energy that we tap into can provide us with inspiration, reassurance, and direction or focus when we need it. If we had to personify this energy, it would take the form of a wise, loving, comforting guiding being... God.

One of the many benefits of this ever-deepening relationship with meditation is that the force of love, wisdom, comfort and inspiration that we tap into can guide us on a path that is consistent with our most loving vision of ourselves. We can receive input and inspiration that enables us to understand our desires and to identify ways that these desires can take form.

Meditation has many benefits in addition to helping you see and erase subconscious blocks to prosperity. For example, meditation can give you a more positive outlook on life, lower your blood pressure, and even reduce the buildup of fatty deposits in your arteries, significantly reducing the risk of heart attack.

Using Meditation

Meditation is simply quieting the mind and body and shutting out the external senses.

When you habitually shut out your external senses, your internal senses become better developed. Just as a blind person has a more acute sense of hearing, an additional awareness develops naturally within you as you practice shutting out your external senses.

You may use these internal senses to unlock useful understanding, memories, and information that have served you, as well as those that have not served you well. This information may help you understand your motivations, your surroundings, and your life. Meditation surrounds you with peace and comfort that you may not realize has been lacking in your life. You receive a sense of safety and security.

In addition, there are the physiological benefits that you receive from the rest and relaxation that comes with meditation. This rest and relaxation can relieve stress and reduce your risk of stress-related illnesses.

Resistance to Meditation

As mentioned previously, our subconscious either drives us toward our outer prosperity or drives us away from it. This is why we examine our subconscious and change any part of it that drives us away from our prosperity.

Meditation is one of the most powerful and effective tools that helps us to discover and examine our conscious and subconscious minds. Meditation is simple, and as easy as breathing, yet the thought of meditating is quite intimidating for many people. Many of us think, almost as a reflex, such thoughts as:

I don't have time to meditate.

I can't concentrate long enough to meditate.

I can't meditate the right way.

There is no right way or wrong way to meditate. There is only the way that yields the results that you desire, so meditation methods need not stand in your way.

We also think that meditation requires discipline, and the thought of discipline triggers subconscious thoughts of punishment, judgment, drudgery and rejection for many of us who have been held to standards of perfection that we could not meet. As a result, we avoid meditation because we don't want to subject ourselves to more discipline.

Developing the habit of meditating requires allowing time for a new habit to replace old habits. These old habits are deeply entrenched, and we are fearful of letting them go because, as described earlier, we believe we need these old habits to survive. Focus on the end result of meditation, and not on the discipline.

Instead of asking:

What if I fail to meditate?

Ask:

What if I succeed in meditating?

Imagine the peace, new awareness, and prosperity that can result. By focusing on the end result and seeing the positive benefits, we are more likely to make room for this new habit.

Use Your Resistance

Resistance to meditation is natural, so don't waste your time judging yourself for resisting. Instead, spend that time and energy appreciating that your resistance is a tool for growth.

When you do weight training, it's the resistance that builds the muscle strength, because resistance causes the blood to flow, bringing the necessary nutrients to the muscles, forming new blood vessels, forming new tissue, and creating the growth that you desire. By the same token, if you use your resistance to meditation as a tool and a motivator, resistance to your good builds your ability to draw your good to you.

Find a Private Meditation Place

To find the right physical place to meditate, choose a place that is quiet and comfortable, a place that makes you feel safe and at home. A dear friend uses her bathroom. She has several children and little privacy, so the only place that works for her is her bathroom. She can close the door, shut out the world and focus on herself.

Emotional release can be quite loud, and you do not want to hold back. When you are engaged in emotional release, in addition to a private place, you will want to find a time and place when you can be loud—for example, when you are alone at home, or in your parked car.

Find the Right Time

It is also useful to choose the right time. Although anytime that works for you can be the right time, I recommend meditating either the first thing in the morning or the last thing in the evening because that is when you have the most control over your time.

Find the Right Position

Many people prefer to meditate seated in a chair with their open palms turned up. This opens you to the powerful energy of the universe. People who practice yoga often take a similar position while seated cross-legged on the floor or on a mat or rug.

Position is a matter of choice and circumstance. Once you become comfortable with meditation, you will find that you can quickly address a surprise situation while standing upright or walking.

Learn to Concentrate

Clear your mind of all extraneous thoughts before meditating. One technique I use is to think back on the things that have happened in the prior twenty-four hours. Then, I think forward to the things I anticipate happening in the next twenty-four hours. By focusing on these things prior to going into deep meditation, I prevent them from popping into my mind as distracting, random thoughts.

After trying to clear my mind, when I found that I still had trouble concentrating and random thoughts were everywhere, I have used the candle technique with much success. Begin by concentrating on a candle and note how long your attention stays on the candle before a random thought enters your mind. You'll find that the more you concentrate on the candle, the longer the intervals become between times that random thoughts enter your mind.

As with any discipline, your ability to concentrate becomes better and stronger with practice. Another technique that I have found effective once you are well practiced in meditation and find yourself *on a roll*, is to simply picture yourself flushing a toilet, and all your daily cares vanish down the drain.

Free Yourself of External Distractions

Choose a quiet meditation place. One of the objectives of meditation is to tune out your external senses so you become more aware of your inner senses.

Choose a dark place that is free of visual distractions. This, of course, can be done by closing your eyes. But you can also darken the room. I started using a blackout mask like the mask airlines give you to help you sleep on overseas flights. The pressure of the mask became more of a physical distraction, so I simply got up and turned out the lights.

To further eliminate physical distractions, ensure that your meditation place is comfortable. Overall, remember that there is no right or wrong way to meditate. Whatever works for you is fine.

Watch What Happens

As you become more attuned to your internal senses, you may find that they become more astute. You may feel things more deeply. You may hear a *still, small voice*. You may get impressions more clearly. You may find that your imagination becomes more vivid. These expanded senses help you gain insights into yourself and into others.

You may find that you understand more than you understood before. For example, I've guided many into the depths of their subconscious where, contrary to their conscious desires, they found deeply held beliefs that they did not deserve their good and that motivated them to take action to thwart their good.

As mentioned earlier, one client who consciously wanted to be well subconsciously believed that the only way she could receive her mother's love was to be sick, and that she would die if she didn't have her mother's nurturing love. Although this is an extreme example of how our subconscious may sabotage our conscious desires, it is clear that we have many events buried in our subconscious minds that may thwart our conscious desires. As you gain more control over your inner senses, you can use them to gain insights, and these insights can give you the information that you need to heal your life, manifest all that you desire, and achieve inner peace and outer prosperity.

Strengthening Your Meditations

We will now conduct an exercise that is designed to help you develop your internal senses more fully. You can practice this and other exercises from memory after reading through them, or you can put your resistance to good use by recording them in your own calm, soothing voice and playing them back as you do the exercises.

Exercise: Developing Your Internal Senses

- In a private meditation place, while seated upright, place your hands in your lap, palms upward.

- Begin by thinking about the things that have happened in the last twenty-four hours and the things that you anticipate happening in the coming twenty-four hours.

- As you move these thoughts out of your mind and your mind becomes clearer, begin to concentrate on your breathing. Breathe deeply. Inhale deeply, and exhale deeply.

- Inhale deeply... and exhale deeply.

- Inhale deeply... and exhale deeply.

- As you continue to inhale and exhale, notice that your breath has a rhythm.

- Focus on the rhythm of your breath.

- Continue to breathe and let your mind focus on your breath. When a random thought pops into your mind, move it back out of your mind. Mentally set it on a shelf and say, *I will deal with you later*, and continue to breathe.

- As you continue to breathe, and as you notice the rhythm of your breath, you become calmer.

- You become more relaxed.

- You begin feeling this relaxation in the top of your head.

- This relaxation flows down around your facial muscles.

- This relaxation flows down the back of your head, almost like warm oil flowing over your body.

- And it relaxes the muscles in the back of your neck.

- This relaxation continues to flow down your body like warm oil, relaxing your shoulders so your shoulders begin to slump.

- This relaxation continues to wash down you, relaxing your chest.

- This relaxation moves down your arms into your hands.

- Your arms and hands are relaxed.

- This relaxation continues to dwell in the area of your chest, and it relaxes your chest.

- You feel a difference in your heart.

- This relaxing energy continues to move down, and it moves down and into your torso.

- This energy touches all of the vital organs housed in your torso.

- This energy continues to relax you.

- This energy now moves into your buttocks and your sexual organs with love and acceptance.

- This energy relaxes that area of your body.

- And you continue to relax.

- This energy moves down into your thighs, and it moves down your calves, and it moves down into your feet, until it moves to the soles of your feet.

- Now, your whole body is relaxed.

- Your whole body is now relaxed.

- Your whole body is now relaxed.

- You are now surrounded with the energy of relaxation. It feels like a warm, wonderful, comforting oil that surrounds your body and relaxes it. With this relaxation you have an expanded perception. You have an expanded awareness. And you use that awareness in this meditation.

- In front of you, you see an orange.

- You examine this fruit and, in your mind's eye, you hold this orange in front of you.

- You examine it with your hand. You turn it over, you look at the navel, you look at the ridges in the skin, you look at the coloring.

- You hold it.

- You feel the weight of the orange. You feel it's texture. And then you feel your body's reaction to the orange.

- Are you salivating more in preparation of eating the orange?

- Do you feel the juices in your stomach flowing?

- To satisfy your hunger, you begin to peel the orange.

- First, you stick your thumb in the navel.

- Notice what it feels like to stick your thumb in the navel of the orange.

- Now you see yourself peeling it.

- See yourself peeling it.

- Feel the juices squirting out of the orange.

- Notice the feeling as the peel tears back from the body of the orange.

- Feel the juice squirting.

- Now feel the juice running down your fingertips.

- Notice the smell of the orange.

- Continue peeling the orange.

- Place the pieces of the orange peel in a pile next to you.

- See the pieces of the orange peel in a pile.

- Now you've completely peeled the orange.

- You have completely peeled the orange.

- See the remnants of the orange rind around the actual body of the orange.

- Separate the orange into its parts.

- Feel the juice from the orange beginning to dry on your fingertips.

- Continue smelling the orange.

- Now, just when you think you are ready to eat the orange, take the pieces of the orange and put them back, so that the orange is now whole.

- You see it just as you did before you separated it into parts.

- You see the remnants of the peel surrounding the orange.

- You see the peel of the orange in a pile next to you.

- Now, take the peel and play the video of you peeling the orange in reverse.

- See yourself putting the peel back on the orange.

- See yourself putting the peel back on the orange, piece by piece.

- You are re-covering the orange.

- Continue to see yourself re-covering the orange until the orange is whole again.

- Feel the disappointment because you were unable to eat the orange as you desired.

- Feel the smoothness of the surface of the orange now that the peel is back on it. Now hold the orange and its wholeness again.

- Continue holding the orange.

- Thank the orange for participating in your journey back to your imagination.

- Now, bring your consciousness back to the here and now and we will continue working.

- You are now situated in the here and now.

- You are fully present here.

Unleash Your Imagination

What we have done is one of many ways of unleashing the imagination within all of us. The imagination gives us the opportunity and the power to begin to see things differently. The imagination gives us the power to begin to see the possibilities in our lives. With the imagination, we can begin to see with a new pair of eyes—our *inner eyes*. We can discern what is true, and what has been told to us that is not true, for what we have learned that is not true keeps us from living with joy, abundance, and peace.

Create Your Concentration Scene

At first, many people have difficulty developing the concentration skills necessary for an effective meditation. Once you learn to use your imagination more effectively, it can increase your ability to concentrate during meditation. You can use your imagination to concentrate on an image that is already familiar to you. We will call this image your *concentration scene*. Your concentration scene can be any image that is already firmly ingrained in your mind's eye.

For example, if you spend a great deal of time driving to and from work, your car windshield right above the dashboard is probably very familiar to you. You could focus on the windshield above the dashboard of your car because that is a picture that pops into your mind quite readily.

Or, you might place an imaginary writing tablet in front of you and focus on a page of this tablet. If you spend a great deal of time staring at a computer, you might choose to focus on the computer's screen saver, because that is a visual image that is firmly planted in your mind's eye. You could also focus on a television screen, or watch a candle flicker.

Exercise: Using Your Concentration Scene

This is a quick exercise that you can repeat frequently to become more comfortable clearing your mind of random thoughts before meditating.

> *As described earlier, actively consider everything that happened in the previous twenty-four hours and everything that you anticipate happening in the next twenty-four hours. This removes many of the random thoughts that could occur. Mentally put these thoughts on a shelf so your mind is clearer than before.*
>
> *After clearing your mind, focus on your concentration scene and see the number one pop onto the scene, then see the number two pop up and so on until you reach the number ten. Take your time and as you count, continue focusing on the screen, embedding that scene in your mind's eye.*
>
> *As you imagine your concentration scene, notice how often a random thought pops into your head.*

At first, random thoughts might be relatively frequent, but as you become more practiced, the interval between random thoughts becomes longer and longer.

Mentally Construct Your Safe Space

When you feel safe and secure, you can concentrate better, and pray and meditate more effectively. You can feel more secure in a mentally constructed safe space. This is not your private, physical meditation *place*, which you have already set up to be comfortable and peaceful. This is your inner space, constructed with the power of your imagination and your creative energies. In preparation for meditation or, optionally, during meditation, construct what you can think of as your *safe space of prayer and meditation.*

Your safe space of prayer and meditation can be mythical or mystical. It can be any place you want it to be. You can surround yourself with things or symbols of things that give you comfort and peace. It can be indoors or outdoors. It can be on a mountain. It can be in a river valley. It can be by a beautiful babbling brook or in a wonderful palatial estate.

You can envision that you have all the tools you need. You can imagine tools that you would need for protection, such as an imaginary bubble to surround you so that you know you are protected. You can create tools for comfort, such as a comfortable bed. You can create tools that you would need for your survival in your space, such as food, water, a printing press to print money, a potter's wheel to form other objects that you desire. You will have your concentration screen so you can see the scenes you might need to see. Spend some time with your imagination constructing this safe space.

In addition to visually painting a picture of your safe space, become acquainted with how you feel when you are in your safe space. When you are meditating, how does the chair feel beneath you? How does the wind feel as it gently, gently, caresses you? What sounds if any do you hear when you are in your safe space? Construct this vision of your safe space and work with it, stay with it, so that if anytime you need to return to your safe space in your mind, that vision is clear, and firmly embedded in your mind.

My Safe Space of Prayer and Meditation

Use the following blank area to construct your safe space. Be sure to include all the tools that you will need to feel safe and secure.

Observing Your Inner Awareness

When you have created your safe space of prayer and meditation, and you have begun to feel more comfortable with the adventure of meditation, you are ready to begin experiencing the fruits of meditation. One of the fruits of meditation is the ability to contact your inner awareness (your conscious and subconscious minds working in harmony) and any subconscious ideas, memories or beliefs that may stand between you and your prosperity. Once you uncover these subconscious roadblocks to your prosperity, you can move them out of the way.

About Me

Below, I have developed two exercises that enable you to observe your inner awareness and assess whether it supports or thwarts your prosperity. Becoming introspective requires patience and practice. During our lives we spend so much time focusing on and responding to our outer world that we rarely take the time to embark on the inner journey to develop the awareness that creates our outer world.

Exercise: About Me #1

This is one of the most crucial parts of your journey. Practice meditating and pondering the questions that it raises. Begin each exercise by relaxing as you did at the beginning of the previous exercise, *Developing Your Internal Senses*. When you come out of your meditative state, write down the first thing that comes to mind in response to the statements in the exercise.

About Me

I feel best when I....

Time seems to stand still when I...

I feel joy when I...

Time seems to drag when I....

These are my loves...

These are my dislikes...

These are my passions...

These are my joys...

Exercise: About Me #1,
with Reasons

Now that you've completed this exercise, perhaps you see why self-awareness takes practice. Note that this next version of the exercise asks you to state *why* you feel or think a certain way. For more clarity, repeat this exercise as many times as you like to refine your answers, using a notebook, tablet, etc. as needed.

About Me

I feel best when I...

because...

Time seems to stand still when I...

because...

I feel joy when I...

because...

Time seems to drag when I...

because...

These are my loves...

because...

These are my dislikes...

because...

These are my passions...

because...

These are my joys...

because...

Examining Your Heart's Desires

The two exercises you just completed can be very powerful in helping you to determine your heart's desires. Notice when your conscious desires are based on your heart's desires and when they are based on what others expect you to be or have expected you to be in the past.

For example, for a large part of my life, I desired business success, and pursued education and career advancement because it was what others expected of me. Of course, there was also a part of me (my ego) that wanted this because I believed that the path of business success was the path to acceptability and love from others.

As I grew, evolved, and achieved the success that I wanted on all levels, I began to wonder:

Is this all there is?

If so, why is there still an empty place within me?

I began to work within myself to find the pathways to prosperity that I share with you now. I realized that there was a new way that I wanted to express and there were new things that I wanted to experience, and these new experiences would bring me the true prosperity that I desired.

This new way, and the new experiences were a *path within*, an inner experience of prosperity. These were not mutually exclusive of my business success. In fact, my business success enabled me to pursue the path within for a deeper experience of prosperity by providing me with the freedom to explore my heart's desire from a place of comfort and peace.

I'm sure I'm not alone in living someone else's agenda for my life and finally wondering:

Is this all there is?

Are my desires my own?

*To what extent have my desires been projected onto me
by others?*

In what ways have you been backed into a corner like the professor who was guided by feedback to cower in a corner of the lecture hall? This inner awareness can help you to be clear in creating your desires based on the deepest self-awareness that creates your prosperity with a clarity that satisfies your soul.

My Beliefs

The next exercise in self-awareness helps you to understand your deepest beliefs. As we established in previous chapters, your beliefs help to shape your experiences. When you understand your beliefs, you can transform any beliefs that create experiences that you no longer wish to have.

Exercise: My Beliefs #1

As with the previous exercises, you will get the most out of this exercise if you begin by entering a state of relaxation as you did at the beginning of the exercise, *Developing Your Internal Senses*.

Write down the first thing that pops into your mind. You don't have to edit your responses or be politically correct, because you are the only one who will see them. Be true to your thoughts and feelings.

My Beliefs

At work I believe that...

I believe that my partner...

I believe that my body...

I believe that sex...

I believe that money...

I believe that power...

I believe that men...

I believe that women...

I believe that children...

I believe that I...

I believe that religion...

I believe that spirituality...

I believe that God...

I believe that my parents...

I believe that my friends...

Examining Your Beliefs

You are not alone if your responses to this exercise surprised you. Most people who are truly candid with themselves, and aware of their inner dialogue, may be surprised that their subconscious beliefs are different from their conscious desires. Since we attract and are attracted to experiences that reflect both our conscious and subconscious beliefs, we can now begin to see why we have at times had experiences that we did not intend.

Although it is reassuring that you are not alone in having subconscious beliefs that may thwart your conscious desires, it is even more reassuring to know that you can change the beliefs that limit you.

Summary

Meditation is a key tool that can help us unlock the subtle ideas that block our prosperity. Despite its many benefits, there is a resistance to meditation which we can overcome when we make this resistance our friend through patience, persistence and purpose. To further realize the benefits and blessings of meditation, and of prosperity, let us now become aware of parts of our subconscious that seek to frustrate our efforts.

CHAPTER 7

MEET YOUR SILENT SABOTEURS

Earlier, we discovered that our consciousness is a huge database that contains all of our conscious and subconscious experiences, memories, thoughts, actions and reactions. Each time we have a new experience, we check it against the database of our old experiences and interpret the new experience based on our memories of the past. Then we expect our new experience to have the same outcome as the past experience. This does not mean that there is any reason for us to expect a better, more fulfilling outcome.

When there is no reason to expect a better outcome, we see no reason to create that better outcome. Instead, we recreate essentially the same experience over and over again. We do this even though the present experience may involve a different set of circumstances, and a different cast of characters. We are magnetically drawn to essentially the same situation and it is drawn to us. Our subconscious mind influences what we create, and we are not aware that our subconscious mind is sabotaging our conscious desires.

As mentioned earlier, as our consciousness forms we are able to process only 2,000 pieces of information of the 4 billion that we receive each second. The vast majority of information that we receive is filtered down to our subconscious minds, and we are not aware of how this information affects our outlook and our decisions. Because we are unaware of the information stored in our subconscious mind, we recreate our new experiences based on our *total* consciousness, not just our conscious awareness. Our subconscious thoughts, beliefs, experiences and perceptions often create the expectations that give birth to our current experiences, keeping us locked in the consciousness and expectations of our past. These subconscious thoughts, beliefs, experiences and perceptions are often in direct opposition to our conscious desires, overriding and sabotaging our conscious desires. These subconscious thoughts, beliefs, experiences and perceptions are the *silent saboteurs* of our prosperity.

When you consider that the vast majority of your consciousness exists beneath your conscious awareness, it is easier to understand how your subconscious mind can undermine your desire for prosperity. Knowing who these silent saboteurs are, and how they thwart your prosperity, can minimize their impact as you move forward on your journey to prosperity.

The Ego

The ego is the dominant part of our subconscious. It creates our silent saboteurs, gives them refuge, and is home to them. It identifies solely with the physical body and with our physical experiences. It perceives only what can be seen, thought, heard, touched, and smelled.

The ego formed as our subconscious developed. It concocted the stories that we tell ourselves, based on its interpretation of our physical experiences. The ego interprets the data from its environment and creates these stories so that we have the information we need to successfully navigate our environment and to survive. For example, in an earlier chapter, a woman created a story based on the ego's interpretation that in order to have the love that she needed to survive, she had to get sick. She formed this interpretation because the only time she got loving attention from her mother was when she was sick. This conditioned her to associate illness with survival in the same way that Pavlov's dogs were conditioned to associate a ringing bell with being fed, and salivated each time they heard the bell ring.

The stories that the ego creates do not consider the influence of the spiritual Source that you connect with in meditation. Because the ego creates these stories without vital information from the Source, its stories tend to be inaccurate. This inaccuracy limits us, keeping us from being the expansive beings we were meant to be, and from having the expansive experiences we were meant to have.

When the ego is in balance with our spiritual selves, it serves a wonderful purpose. It helps us survive in our physical environment. However, because the ego is solely physical, not taking into account our spiritual selves, its perceptions are often unbalanced. Consider again how as a child we are at the mercy of our environment. We have no means of protection, nurturing, or sustenance. We are totally dependent on those outside of ourselves for survival. As we grow older, we may be vaguely aware of a force, an energy, a *something* that is bigger than us. We may even feel this energy profoundly at times when our needs for survival are met. As a result, we may feel at peace and content. However, in times of need, distress, or lack, our attention turns to the people, stimuli and factors that we depend upon for our survival.

As adults, the survival techniques that worked as children sabotage our well-being, unless we learn a new way. As more of our attention focuses on the people, stimuli and circumstances outside of us, we neglect and discount the life force within and around us, the life force that gives us a feeling of peace. Our subconscious believes that the outside world is more vital to our existence, and it ignores the internal and external energies that would fill us with a sense of well-being and attract our needs and wishes to us.

How we see ourselves depends on how our environment reacts to us, and we lose sight of our connection to a great Source of power and support. We believe that our survival is so dependent on external sources that we forget that the magnetic power of our internal force can be a useful tool that attracts our experiences to us and draws us to these experiences. As a result, our own creative power and potential diminish in the same way that any talent we don't use diminishes. We believe that we are at the mercy of our environment, and that we must mold our self-image accordingly in order to get what we need to survive.

A woman I counseled provides an example of how the ego can be self-destructive when it is out of balance. When interviewing for a new job, she believed that for the job to be acceptable she had to have a certain title. She found the perfect job, with the perfect commute, perfect compensation, perfect uses of her skills and perfect potential for additional growth and development. However, the job didn't come with the title that her ego demanded. Subconsciously, her ego concocted the story that she would be socially acceptable and get the admiration that she needed to survive only if she had the title of Vice President. She insisted on the job title, negotiations broke down, and the job offer was rescinded. If her ego had been in balance with an inner sense of self-love, she would have been less insistent on the outward affirmation of a specific job title and could have avoided this self-destructive experience.

Through meditation, we can reconnect the ego with the Source of creativity, power and grace. This balances the ego which, when brought into balance, is a good thing. It is simply a physical survival tool that can be paired with our spiritual tools of survival so we can thrive and reclaim the prosperity that is our natural birthright.

So you can better understand the complexity of the ego, I have characterized different parts of the ego as your silent saboteurs, who would thwart your journey to prosperity. Each of these silent saboteurs is based on the fear that you will not get what you need to survive.

The Inner Judge

The inner judge is afraid of failure. It sees the world through the prism of past negative experiences that have caused us pain, shame, fear, embarrassment, humiliation, uncertainty and doubt. Its primary motivation is to avoid another negative experience. The inner judge often repeats the mantra:

What if I fail?

This inner chatter keeps us from trying something new, considering a different approach, or stretching ourselves to achieve our fullest potential. The inner judge causes us to reject a suggestion out of hand, or holds us back from something that we really want. Subconsciously, we are hypnotized by fear of failure, and there is no room in our subconscious for a vision of success that would propel us forward toward prosperity.

Through prayer and meditation, we can teach our inner judge a new truth by giving ourselves a different experience so the inner judge can use its powers of discernment to recognize when the universe is supporting us completely and unconditionally.

The Inner Critic

Whereas the debilitating mission of the inner judge is to avoid negative external experiences, the inner critic is that subconscious voice that tells us everything that is wrong with us. In subconscious conversations with ourselves, we say things to ourselves so hateful that we wouldn't dare utter these thoughts to another person. However, these utterances lurk right beneath the surface of our consciousness like sharks lurking beneath murky water, and attack our conscious desires.

The inner critic is the most visible aspect of our ego because its voice often bubbles to the surface into our conscious awareness. It often echoes comments, statements and reactions that we heard in the past and uses those experiences against us, convincing us of our mistakes, unworthiness, weakness, incompetence, and the futility of any effort to create the joy that we truly desire. It echoes the feedback that we've received from our outer world and plays out a cycle of frustration over and over again.

I observed the debilitating effects of the inner critic one day when a very petite client arrived early for her appointment just as my prior client, who was obese, was leaving. My petite client was so upset at the sight of my obese client that she could not concentrate on the issues that had brought her to see me until we discussed her strong reaction to my obese client. It soon became clear that she was reliving the withering pain caused by the criticism of her mother, who had always insisted that she watch her weight or she might never attract the love she needed from a man. The implied threat from her mother was that if she didn't have a man's love, she wouldn't have what she needed to survive. This was one of many harsh criticisms from her mother that left her unable to finish projects, make strong emotional connections, or find satisfaction in any of her other pursuits due to her fear of criticism. As we talked, she became aware of repressed memories of how she had been harshly criticized, how deeply she feared criticism, and how her fear of criticism kept her from opening herself to the intimacy that she desired.

The inner critic sometimes speaks so loudly and clearly that we feel unable to silence it, in which case the old saying, *If you can't beat 'em, join 'em* is appropriate. If the voice of the inner critic rings so loudly in your subconscious that you can't silence it, then you can redeploy it to dissect information so you can discern the truth in any situation.

You can redeploy your inner critic by turning its criticism into discernment, and by finding yourself completely acceptable so you can accept your good.

The Inner Saint

The inner saint is the ego-based subconscious belief that there is a perfect way to do everything, a perfect way to be, and a perfect experience that we must seek in order to deserve your good.

The inner saint is held hostage by the paradox of perfection, which says as described earlier, *I am imperfect and therefore I don't deserve my good.* Such mythical standards of perfection are based on ignorance of biology, sanitation and such, and have been espoused as the standards to which we should all aspire. We learned to measure our behavior against these mythical standards and, due to this comparison, we developed a consciousness of guilt because we believed that we would not receive God's blessing and, thus, what we need to survive. These standards of perfection cannot be met.

Lurking in the subconscious mind, the inner saint paints a picture of what perfection *should* look like. The inner saint has been influenced by mass media and the portrayals of perfection that it has seen. It takes mental snapshots of media images that portray the perfect body type, job, family, home, and personality. It then imagines how things should happen or how an experience should play out. When our experiences don't look like they're *supposed* to look, we feel unworthy of our good and we subconsciously reject what we consciously want.

The inner saint has made an arrangement with the universe for conditional love, where the inner saint expects the blessings of the universe only if the exacting conditions of the inner saint are met. Until confronted, the inner saint edges out our awareness of the unconditional love that flows to us and through us when we move into the meditative spiritual practices that align us with the Higher Power. This energy of unconditional love surrounds us and is activated within us regardless of our judgments, criticisms or the way things look. Through prayer and meditation, we can teach the inner saint that it is loved no matter how things look. It does not have to be afraid of being punished if reality differs from the idealized view it has created.

Any mother who has gone into a grocery with a child and entered an aisle filled with candy has experienced her inner saint. She enters the store with the high hopes constructed by her inner saint that her child will be well-behaved because her ego sees her as a good mother, and a good mother has well-behaved children. Her child has learned that it can get what it believes it needs to survive by crying and creating a disturbance. The child has also observed that the good mother is especially responsive when out in public, so the child strategically creates a disruption in public because the desired response is almost guaranteed. Like clockwork, the good mother, who has an ego investment in how she is seen, responds to the child by buying candy, because she believes that a good mother would not ignore the cries of the child, and would not have a child who misbehaves in public. The child behaves as it is programmed to behave. When the child gets what it wants, it is calm, the grocery store is more profitable, and the good mother's ego-need to be viewed in a certain way is satisfied.

We can teach our subconscious mind to suspend its belief that it will be punished if the actual experience differs from the idealized experience. We do this in the same way that we allow our minds to suspend disbelief when we see an actor play a historic figure. In reality, we know the historic figure didn't look like the actor, and we are willing to release the idea that the movie and the reality must match. By the same token, in order to have peace and move forward toward our desires, we suspend the demand that our reality must match the movie created by the inner saint.

The Inner Sinner

The inner saint described above sits on the left shoulder of a person contemplating an action. The inner sinner sits on the right shoulder, and these two competing parts of the ego cancel out the forward progress that you want to make toward your prosperity. This cartoonish image became a cliché because these competing energies are so prevalent in our minds that we all understand the image.

The inner sinner follows the soul's impulsive attraction to joy, fulfillment and the full experience of life's offerings. This aspect of our subconscious mind is often judged to be hedonistic when compared to the Judeo-Christian, puritanical obsession with martyrdom, self-denial and an austere experience to be rewarded later in heaven.

This judgment that the inner sinner is hedonistic causes subconscious guilt that contributes to the destruction of our dreams. When we observe the enterprising nature of a child, we see that the child wants to explore everything, experience everything, and follow the impulses of the moment. As we come to realize this, we understand that our inherent curiosity and openness to our earthly experience are natural.

However, just as a child's enterprising spirit is suppressed by the practical need for safety, the soul's desire for fulfillment is suppressed by the puritanical restrictions of the Judeo-Christian consciousness. When this suppression creates imbalance, the soul's natural desires become distorted and we act out in ways that are ultimately counterproductive. This acting out perpetuates the consciousness of guilt that creates an energy of unworthiness, and we can't consciously create what we subconsciously believe we don't deserve.

We can deploy the energies of the inner sinner in a balanced and productive way so these energies are not suppressed in a way that creates destructive patterns. When the naturally enterprising energies of the inner sinner are suppressed, it acts out in similarly damaging and distorted ways, perpetuating the consciousness of guilt.

For example, in college I observed two friends who had two completely different experiences with drinking. For one friend, alcohol had always been the forbidden fruit that had great allure. As soon as he was away from home, he went on drinking binges followed by destructive behavior that damaged his relationships, damaged school property and damaged his reputation. The other

THE SOUL OF PROSPERITY

friend had been taken to pubs, had been allowed to drink wine with dinner for several years, and had learned a healthy respect for the power of alcohol. He was able to integrate alcohol consumption into his life with a balance that maintained his wellbeing without the destructive behavior of my other friend.

The Inner Child

Guilt sabotages prosperity.

Given the many characterizations of the ego that dwell in our subconscious mind, is it any wonder that prosperity has eluded us? At this point, it may seem that the saboteurs of prosperity are as numerous and varied as the leaves falling from the trees in autumn, and equally difficult to clean up. However, we can begin to manage our subconscious mind by becoming aware of that part of our subconscious that lies at the root of our ego: the inner child.

Many parts of our subconscious mind, such as the inner judge and the inner critic, were formed in our childhood. Feelings of rejection, memories of shame, and painful childhood experiences form lasting impressions, crystallizing in the habitual thought patterns that characterize the silent saboteurs. By retraining the inner child's feelings of fear, inadequacy, shame, doubt, and failure, we can overcome our silent saboteurs.

The inner child still sees itself as a helpless child at an earlier stage of psychological, physical, and spiritual development. It has learned such stories as, *I must have an illness in order to have the love that I need to survive.*

Our inner child is clearly irrational when we examine it from the perspective of an objective, rational adult. However, our inner child has been so traumatized and hypnotized by its prior experiences that it cannot see clearly. It has also developed such brilliant coping mechanisms that its actions, reactions and responses hide stealthily beneath the surface of our awareness, so we don't even know that it is operating. We've all experienced ourselves acting out the unmet needs of the inner child.

I was once reminded how easily we can revert to an old consciousness that we thought we had dealt with when a client discussed his experience at his class reunion. Although he and his peers had been out of high school for forty years, one of the nuns who had taught them had been invited to give brief remarks. They didn't realize that she was senile, and she talked for almost two hours. The organizers were frozen, unable to regain control of the program to resume the other activities they had scheduled. Although collectively they rationalized that this was due to respect, they had all reverted to their childhood reverence for and obedience to authority, which the nun symbolized. Guilt was so deeply locked in their subconscious that they were unable to assert their adult power.

We often revert to behavior that defies reason due to the emotional wounds inflicted in childhood. We rarely notice when we revert to illogical behavior because our consciousness has become quite adept at rationalizing behaviors that enable us to ignore the feelings that lurk beneath the surface of our consciousness and *really* drive our behavior. The gateway to these feelings is our inner child.

We begin our process of healing and transformation by healing the inner child.

To heal your inner child, use your safe inner space of prayer and meditation to retrain it and repeatedly expose it to the essential energy of love and acceptance it needs in order to see itself and the world differently.

Once the inner child feels safe and secure, give it permission to speak. Its wisdom, power, grace, beauty, courage and creativity will astound you. This is the part of you that has been taught of its limits, and thus has forgotten its unlimited nature. This is the part of you that has been taught of its inadequacy and has been unable to see or create the potential for its good that has always existed. This is also the part of you that is filled with courage so deep that it will amaze you when you unharness it, so innocent that it does not understand guilt or punishment. Your inner child is and has always been connected with the life force and the divine purpose and potential for your life and, once unharnessed, it goes forward fearlessly and effortlessly.

Meet Your Inner Child

The following exercise will give you a chance to hone your meditation skills so you can use meditation to get in touch with your subconscious mind, and the erroneous stories that contributed to the creation of your silent saboteurs. Optionally, as with the prior meditation exercises, you can read and remember these exercises, or record the words in your own voice and use the recording to move into a meditative state.

This exercise will help you relax and enter a place of deeper inner awareness. It also provides you with a template that you can use to meet your inner child. Later, you can use this template to meet and transform your other silent saboteurs so they can support your journey to prosperity instead of sabotaging it. Eventually, you can use this template to recognize and remove any obstacles in the pathways to your inner prosperity.

Exercise: Meet Your Inner Child

You begin this meditation by practicing the art of relaxation. You will then descend to the bottom of a staircase comprised of ten steps. When you get to the bottom of the stairs, you will find yourself in a pool of warm water, as if you're in a Jacuzzi. Or, if you prefer, you can find yourself in the safe space that you have created for yourself. It doesn't matter. This pool of warm water or the safe space that you have created will surround you with a sense of peace, safety, comfort and your inherent spirituality. In this space you will know yourself to be more than just your physical body.

Let us begin.

Stage 1: Relaxation.

- Ten times, Inhale deeply, and exhale deeply. Each time as you inhale and exhale, listen to your breath. Focus only on your breath. Concentrate all of your thoughts and all of your energy on your breath. Let your breath hypnotize you as you continue to breathe. Let yourself relax into the rhythm of your breath.

- Focus all of your attention and energy on the tips of your toes, and feel your toes and feet begin to relax.

- Continue to breathe and have the thought:

    I give my toes and feet permission to relax.

    I give my toes and feet permission to relax.

    I give my toes and feet permission to relax.

- Continue to breathe and become aware of your toes and feet, and how much more relaxed they are.

- Continue to breathe and have the thought:

  I give my calves, shins and thighs permission to relax.

  I give my calves, shins and thighs permission to relax.

  I give my calves, shins and thighs permission to relax.

- Continue to breathe and become aware of your calves, shins, and thighs, and how much more relaxed they are.

- Continue to breathe, and have the thought:

  I give my hips and buttocks permission to relax.

  I give my hips and buttocks permission to relax.

  I give my hips and buttocks permission to relax.

- Continue to breathe and become aware of your hips and buttocks, and how much more relaxed they are.

- Continue to breathe, and have the thought:

  I give my torso and internal organs permission to relax.

  I give my torso and internal organs permission to relax.

  I give my torso and internal organs permission to relax.

- Continue to breathe and become aware of your torso and internal organs, and how much more relaxed they are.

- Continue to breathe and have the thought:

  I give my chest and heart permission to relax.

  I give my chest and heart permission to relax.

  I give my chest and heart permission to relax.

- Continue to breathe and become aware of your chest and heart, and how much more relaxed they are.

- Continue to breathe and have the thought:

  I give my shoulders, arms and hands permission to relax.

  I give my shoulders, arms and hands permission to relax.

  I give my shoulders, arms and hands permission to relax.

- Continue to breathe and become aware of your shoulders, arms and hands, and how much more relaxed they are.

- Continue to breathe and have the thought:

  I give my neck, face and head permission to relax.

  I give my neck, face and head permission to relax.

  I give my neck, face and head permission to relax.

- Continue to breathe and become aware of your neck, face and head, and how much more relaxed they are.

Stage 2: Entering the Subconscious Mind.

- Now that you are relaxed, imagine that you are at the top of a set of stairs, and breathe deeply. Know that with each step you take, you will feel better, more comfortable and more relaxed.

- Step down from Step 10 to Step 9 and breathe deeply. Take a moment to get comfortable on Step 9, continuing to breathe.

- Step down from Step 9 to Step 8 and breathe deeply. Take a moment to get comfortable on Step 8, continuing to breathe.

- Step down from Step 8 to Step 7 and breathe deeply. Take a moment to get comfortable on Step 7, continuing to breathe.

- Step down from Step 7 to Step 6 and breathe deeply. Take a moment to get comfortable on Step 6, continuing to breathe.

- Step down from Step 6 to Step 5 and breathe deeply. Take a moment to get comfortable on Step 5, continuing to breathe.

- You're halfway there. Take a moment to reflect on how good you feel. Take a moment to anticipate how much better you will feel when you get to the bottom of the stairs and into your safe space, or into the pool of warm, welcoming water that will comfort and support you.

- Step down from Step 5 to Step 4 and breathe deeply. Take a moment to get comfortable on Step 4, continuing to breathe.

- Step down from Step 4 to Step 3 and breathe deeply. Take a moment to get comfortable on Step 3, continuing to breathe.

- Step down from Step 3 to Step 2 and breathe deeply. Take a moment to get comfortable on Step 2, continuing to breathe.

- Step down from Step 2 to Step 1 and breathe deeply. Take a moment to get comfortable on Step 1, continuing to breathe.

Stage 3: Entering your safe space.

Now you are ready to enter your safe inner space and use your concentration scene. You will repeat the process of descending to this safe space regularly. You will become increasingly comfortable coming here, and you will become increasingly able to arrive here more quickly whenever you choose.

- Step down from Step 1 and enter your safe space, or the pool of peaceful, loving warm liquid in the Jacuzzi. Concentrate on how loved and supported you feel. Take a moment to relax in this safe, loving space. Spend as much time as you want to spend here.

- Now, see your concentration scene in front of you. It can be a movie screen, a flat screen TV or any kind of screen that you choose.

- When this view is firmly embedded in your mind, ask to see the vision of yourself that is most appropriate for the moment. You will probably see yourself as a young child.

- Ask:

  What is the child wearing?

  Who is the child with?

  What are the circumstances surrounding this child?

  How is the child feeling?

- Take a few moments to make a mental note of this child and its circumstances.

Stage 4: Conversations with your Subconscious Mind.

When you have repeated this exercise over and over and are comfortable going this far, then you will continue by just lovingly observing the child.

- Now, when you've had a chance to contemplate this child from your safe space of love, power, peace and healing, project healing energy onto this child. Do this simply by imagining that the feelings of love, peace, power, grace and healing that surround you take the form of white light and flow to the child. This white light surrounds the screen and surrounds the child.

- Ask the child what it needs. Don't be alarmed if the child runs, stands silent, or is reluctant to appear. You will repeat this exercise many times until the child learns to trust that the experience will be loving.

- Continue to send loving energy to this child.

- When the child is ready, it will express what it is feeling, and will begin to express its needs.

- Just listen, continuing to send loving energy to the vision of this child.

- The child may need to express repressed emotions. Let it express these repressed emotions.

- If you feel these repressed emotions welling up within your physical body, feel free to use sound, rhythmic actions such as drumming on a pillow, or body movements to let this energy flow from you. It has been locked in your body for decades.

- Continue to feel yourself and the child surrounded in the white light of loving energy.

- Let yourself and your child receive this white light of loving energy as long as you need to.

- To end the conversation, simply exit your safe space and slowly ascend the staircase, one step at a time, pausing briefly on each step to breathe in and out, absorb the experience, and return to your conscious mind.

The next chapter will give you more experience with all parts of your subconscious mind. Return to this exercise and similar ones over and over to create a safe environment for your inner child and for your other silent saboteurs to enable you to unlock the subconscious obstacles to your prosperity. We will repeatedly enter your subconscious mind and give your inner child and your silent saboteurs a safe place to express, objectively listening to their irrational thoughts, and replacing these thoughts with rational thoughts so you can take conscious actions to mitigate the subconscious desire to sabotage what you consciously want.

CHAPTER 8

SILENCING YOUR SABOTEURS

We are often ruled by emotions that are based on fear due to our prior experiences, and these emotions overrule our rational minds. We avoid the potential for pain, and by default we avoid the potential for fulfillment. These emotions are often subconscious, which is why we sometimes act in ways that our rational minds cannot justify.

One way to begin to identify these subconscious emotions is to give them the forms of the silent saboteurs that you met in the previous chapter. Now we will further explain each saboteur and suggest the principal approaches for transforming them.

Transforming Your Ego

As stated before, the ego is the part of our subconscious that identifies solely with the human body and our current experiences. It is that deeply instinctive part that has ingrained programming for its survival. It has developed coping mechanisms to survive, but these same coping mechanisms sabotage our intentions because they are out of balance.

For example, a child cries to communicate its need for food, water, or a diaper change and to avoid discomfort, rashes, and the potential for infection. We learn to create a fuss in order to get attention, and we learn to associate attention with getting the love that we need to survive. However, as adults, many of the ways that we have learned to create a fuss are counterproductive to our intentions.

A person who continually creates a fuss in the workplace can be labeled a trouble maker, which impedes her ability to get ahead and create the professional prosperity that she desires. The person who picks a fight with a potential partner as a cry for love may actually drive that partner away instead of creating the loving relationship he desires.

In each of these instances, the same response that created a productive result in childhood now creates a counterproductive result. The response that was in balance with the need for survival as a child is now out of balance with what is needed as an adult.

As adults in a highly developed society, our survival is rarely at risk. However, subconsciously, when we feel that to survive we need love—or love's proxies, such as attention, respect, etc.—we may *think* subconsciously that our lives are threatened, and our responses are out of proportion to our needs. The ego creates a disproportionate and counterproductive response, so we bring the ego back into balance with the truth of the moment. To do so, it is helpful to further understand the ego.

The ego is simply our instinctive survival mechanism.

The ego has become ingrained in primal fear due to eons of evolution, most of which occurred when the earth was a hostile place for humans, and human survival was constantly at risk.

When humans initially inhabited the earth, they were spiritual beings, unaware of what was necessary to survive the primitive, hostile territory. To survive, they developed instinctive responses, such as a hypervigilance against threats. Eventually, even minor triggers such as a social slight became associated with a deep need for love and survival. This out of balance ego clouded the way they saw the world and edged out the inherent, spiritual awareness that the universe could be a supportive and loving place, and they could see the world in a different, more reasoned way.

The ego was and still is a good thing when it is in balance with our innate spiritual knowledge and we can experience the universe as a loving, supportive place. However, the ego is rarely in balance because it has run amok for eons. That is why healing and balancing the ego is a repetitive process where we teach the silent saboteurs a different way of seeing the world.

This process is not unlike taming a lion. The lion tamer doesn't destroy the lion or fight with it to teach it a new behavior. The ego serves a valuable purpose. When in balance with our inner, spiritual awareness, it helps us to navigate through life. Instead of fighting with it, we want to teach it a new way.

Your task is to invite the ego into your safe meditation space, where you can reconnect it with the Source of creativity, power and grace. This grace balances the influence of the ego.

Redeploying Your Inner Judge

Your inner judge has honed its skills by finding the potential for pain that creates fear in any situation. It has gathered and catalogued all the difficult experiences in your life in a highly intelligent way. It often refers to this database of experiences and uses it to avoid any potential for pain and suffering when it observes anything that reminds it of a past situation that caused pain.

Unfortunately, your inner judge is so busy avoiding pain that it also avoids the potential for pleasure. For example, your inner judge may avoid a potential relationship with someone because that person reminds you of someone in your past with whom you had a challenging relationship. One reason that this reminder is drawn to you is so you can heal the pain of the past relationship and move forward with a more loving experience.

You can teach your inner judge a new truth by giving yourself a different experience. However, the inner judge would rather avoid the disappointment of the prior relationship and hold onto the old story, because the old story is comfortable and familiar. You may have subconsciously adopted this old story as a part of who you believe yourself to be, and it may have garnered sympathy that you equated with love. You may be reluctant to release this old story even when your inner judge compares it to any new situation.

The inner judge is brilliant when it comes to keeping you from your prosperity, but you can retrain your inner judge to use its brilliance to accept the prosperity that is waiting for you. The brilliance of the inner judge is its ability to discern the essence of a situation based on past experiences and past stories.

We can teach the inner judge to reassess a situation based on a new set of maxims.

For example, a woman's inner judge may have experienced men as unreliable and untrustworthy, and she subconsciously believes that any new situation will recreate the same disappointments. The inner judge may have been programmed to selectively perceive only data that matches its beliefs, and screen out information that differs from the maxims (truths) that it knows.

Giving Your Inner Judge the Gift of Truth

Your task is to teach your inner judge a new set of maxims that it can compare to the information inherent in any new situation. When the data matches the new set of maxims, the inner judge will move you forward toward your prosperity instead of resisting it. For example, a woman might actively review instances where men have been trustworthy and reliable and, in doing so, program herself to see any evidence of this reliability that might exist in her new situation.

The old maxims that the inner judge has held are:

> *God doesn't love me. He judges me as imperfect.*
> *Therefore, I don't deserve my good.*

> *The universe doesn't support me. It punishes and*
> *withholds from me, creating lack and struggle.*

> *I don't love myself. Therefore, I don't deserve my good.*

You can teach the inner judge during prayer and meditation and at other times by repeating the affirmations:

> *God loves me completely and unconditionally.*

> *The universe supports me completely and*
> *unconditionally.*

> *I love myself completely and unconditionally.*

These affirmations can create a foundation for a new consciousness that supports your prosperity and also quiets one of your other silent saboteurs, your inner critic.

Calming Your Inner Critic

Your inner critic has been held hostage to the paradox of perfection. As you remember, the paradox of perfection is based on the idea that there is some impossible standard of perfection that we must meet in order to be worthy of God's love. If we feel unworthy of God's love, we feel unworthy of our prosperity, and we subconsciously block our good.

The inner critic finds something unacceptable about every situation. For example, you may shy away from an intimate relationship for fear that the person may see the real you and reject you because your inner critic tells you that you are not acceptable. Your inner critic may conjure up criticisms of your potential partner to blind you to the truth that you are criticizing yourself. It may even make these criticisms seem larger than life in order to put distance between you and your potential partner, or to set up unrealistic expectations or impossible tests for them to pass that give you an excuse to reject your partner before he or she rejects you.

Teach acceptance to your inner critic. In the prior example, the real lesson was to teach you that your subconscious criticisms of another are really places within yourself that you believe are unacceptable. When you find places within you unacceptable, you feel unworthy of the prosperity that you say you want, and this inner criticism sabotages your good.

This path of acceptance begins when you are able to accept your outer circumstances as they are and move forward with them to where you would like to be.

Teaching Your Inner Critic Acceptance, Objectivity and Forgiveness

Your task is to redeploy your inner critic by turning its criticism into discernment, and by finding yourself completely acceptable so that you can accept your good.

To minimize your inner critic's ability to reject your good, you teach it to accept what it has previously found to be unacceptable. This journey into acceptance requires taking an objective view of the situation and applying forgiveness.

In the earlier example, it was very tempting to fixate on your partner's shortcomings. That fixation causes you to miss the true lesson and opportunity for growth, which was that these outer criticisms were simply reflections of things within you that you found to be unacceptable. Their criticism, judgment and disrespect were outward reflections of your unconscious criticism, judgment and disrespect for yourself.

There may be many situations in your life where you felt victimized, unloved, unaccepted or harmed. Many of these cannot be changed, yet you have found them to be unacceptable. You may even have become so accustomed to your victimization that you are unwilling to give it up because, subconsciously, victimization has come to define you. As a result, it requires some effort to move into acceptance. Acceptance does not mean that you condone destructive behavior.

> *Acceptance* *is the willingness to look at a situation*
> *without judgment or criticism, and to choose a path that*
> *leads to peace.*

Acceptance is reconciling yourself to a situation as it exists, without the stress or pressure of needing to change it. When you are accepting, you are ready to say:

> *OK, this happened. I acknowledge it. I will not dwell on it*
> *in a victim mentality, but I will see the lesson, growth*
> *and healing that may come as a result of this situation.*

This is a very tall order, so you can move from the comfortable cocoon of judgment, blame and looking outside yourself to the new place of inner awareness and self-responsibility. Often, it is more comfortable to hold a grudge than to hold the mirror up to ourselves to see the lesson to be learned.

To make this move, enter your safe inner space of prayer and meditation where you are safe creating change. In your safe space, you are adept at bringing in the light that heals the wounds that have lurked in the depths of your subconscious. In your safe space, you can heal this old pain by releasing it into the light of God's love that you draw to yourself. God's love will move into these wounded places in your subconscious and you will feel a sense of love and peace that opens you to the blessing of seeing the situation more objectively instead of seeing it through the prism of your pain.

When you work in this way, you attain an inner state of forgiveness. You realize that forgiveness is not something that you give to another, or to yourself.

> ***Forgiveness*** *is an inner state that you achieve when you feel surrounded, healed and buoyed by God's love, and that love is applied to your inner wounds.*

It is through the process of *salvation* that we experience forgiveness.

> ***Salvation*** *is the application of the salve of God's love to the wounds of your soul.*

Salvation places you in a state of peace, where you are able to see things differently, and where you feel the love that your soul has yearned to experience.

For example, I have worked with many people who have found it difficult to forgive an abusive, alcoholic father who was either unsupportive or absent. These wounds have run deep and have had a lasting impact on some clients' lives. Many had actually gotten comfortable in their victim mentality and it defined the way they saw the world, especially when the same patterns repeated over and over again. When they opened these wounds to receive the healing grace of God's love, I witnessed a new energy, a new perception and a new sense of peace and balance based on their seeing the situation more objectively. Pretty unanimously, they become aware of the father's pain, confusion and turmoil.

This has often occurred after emotional release, the cathartic process of briefly expressing the pain of the old wounds they have suppressed, and releasing this pain to the healing grace of God so it is lifted from them and transformed. They were able to have compassion for their father and for themselves in a way that they were unable to when they were blaming themselves and him for their pain. This powerful transformation, fueled by the objectivity of grace, put them in a state of forgiveness for themselves and for others. From the place of forgiveness, they were able to see the situation more objectively, and to open themselves to the lesson of healing.

With the gift of objectivity, you can see the lesson or healing that is available to you so this lesson or healing can move you closer to your goal. Acceptance may require being able to see a situation in a different way. Acceptance requires a deep understanding and practice of knowing this:

> If you cannot change the choices, decisions or paths of
> others, you can change the way you see things so that
> their choices do not diminish your sense of well-being.

Acceptance requires healing the hurt that the situation has created. Acceptance of others and of situations also requires an acceptance of yourself and a forgiveness of yourself for the pain that you experienced as a result of your prior thinking.

Balancing the Inner Saint and Inner Sinner

The inner saint and inner sinner have been just as imprisoned by the paradox of perfection as the inner critic.

The inner saint believes that it must cling to an impossible standard of perfection in order to earn God's love. The inner saint must accept that the standard of perfection to which it ascribes is just a myth so it can accept itself without condition. The inner saint would starve you when it is out of balance. When it is in acceptance, it will guide you to the most self-loving choices.

The inner sinner believes that its indulgence (food, alcohol, sex, shopping, etc.) will bring it a sense of loving peace. The inner sinner sees its indulgences as substitutes for the love that it seeks. The inner sinner would have you eat a whole gallon of ice cream.

When these two are in balance, you eat what you wish, or indulge in moderation in what brings you joy for balanced and self-loving reasons. The inner saint feels that it must limit the excesses of the inner sinner. The inner sinner has been in a frantic search for what it perceives to be the life-giving force that it needs to survive.

For example, many have learned to subconsciously equate sexual expression with the parental love we believe that we need to survive. As a result, many may be drawn to excessive sexual expression and choices that ultimately are not self-loving because this sexual expression is a substitute for the love that the soul desires. This is prevalent among adolescent girls who become sexually active before they develop the maturity to make self-affirming choices. The conflict between the inner saint and the inner sinner creates the guilt that causes us to withhold our good. In the example of a teenage girl, these choices and the guilt they induce can create consequences such as teen pregnancy, limited life choices, and an unsupportive environment that could last a lifetime if not addressed.

Acceptance will bring peace to these two silent saboteurs. When they are in balance, you will accept your desire for fulfillment as natural, and use the wisdom of the inner saint to guide you to the pursuits that offer you self-loving fulfillment.

To balance the inner saint and inner sinner:

- Teach the inner saint that it is loved no matter how things look so it does not have to be afraid of being punished if reality differs from the idealized view it has created;

- Deploy the energies of the inner sinner in a balanced and productive way so its energies are not suppressed in a way that creates destructive patterns.

Embracing Your Inner Child

A key aspect of the ego is the inner child. As stated earlier, the inner child learned in childhood how to survive and get what it needed. Unfortunately, these lessons, the impressions they left and the rules of engagement they established now sabotage our desires. These life lessons were ingrained early and are deeply embedded in the child's subconscious mind. For example, the child learned conditional love instead of unconditional love when parents threatened to withhold love if the child misbehaved. The child then modified its behavior to conform to standards that would garner positive reinforcement.

Creating positive reinforcement became so routine that it became a part of our subconscious patterning. We are unaware of these responses in the same way that the college professor was unaware that he was forced to one corner of the lecture hall, yet these responses keep us from making the rational adult responses that an objective observer would expect. A child's memories, experiences, pain and fear promote the behavior that a rational adult would reject.

The inner child holds the key to our self-sabotaging behaviors. It is the invisible hand that pushes us forward into behaviors and actions that are self-limiting at best and self-destructive in their extreme. Often, we find ourselves in a situation where we think:

How did I get here?

Or:

I thought I already dealt with that.

When we think these things, it's because of the reactions and responses embedded in our minds from our most formative experiences, and the stories that these experiences taught us. It's as if the energy that drives our behaviors is not adult, rational energy but the unhealed energy of the inner child, and this energy drives us into ditch after ditch, leaving us wondering:

How did I get so far off track?

For example, one of my clients was preparing to be married and to move in with the man of her dreams. However, she became aware of a strong resistance to marriage, which was one of her life-long dreams, and she inexplicably took actions that seemed to sabotage the very things that she had dreamed about. As she anticipated the arrival of her wedding dress, she began to gain weight instead of losing it, despite her dieting. She picked fights with her fiancé prior to moving in with him, and she squandered money they had saved to build their dream house on land they had already purchased. She was mystified, but she knew that the answers were buried somewhere in her childhood, so she decided to meet with me.

As I worked with her, she discovered that, as a child, she moved in the fourth grade. When she got to her new school she was teased mercilessly, called ugly and stupid and tormented by other children. Her home situation was not much better. Her parents ridiculed her for being skinny and being a tomboy who liked the outdoors. They showed a strong preference for her brother, who was overweight.

As we unlocked these childhood memories, it became clear to my client that her inner child was sabotaging her adult desires. Her inner child was terrified and was doing everything it could to stop the move so she wouldn't experience the wrenching pain that she associated with moving. This pain was still buried deep within her subconscious, and avoiding this pain was more important to the inner child than seeking the joy of union was to the rational adult.

In addition, her inner child associated being skinny with being rejected by her parents because she still held painful memories of when her parents rejected her as skinny and preferred her brother, who was heavy. Her inner child resisted losing weight despite her adult desire to fit into her wedding dress. Her inner child associated the parents' love with life itself. Out of an irrational fear that she would lose her parents' love and, thus, the life force itself, her inner child had a primal fear of losing weight.

Through a series of processes, we worked together to reclaim, embrace, love and heal her inner child. By telling the child of her loveliness, worthiness and goodness, and by continually embracing the inner child, she was able to trust that loving things could happen if she let herself move forward.

We have believed that we have had to control our inner child, beat it into submission, or destroy it. But our inner child wants to survive. It resists, and its determination only intensifies when we oppose it. Our attempts to control the involuntary tendency toward self-destructive behaviors causes us to criticize ourselves and to subconsciously withhold our good as punishment, creating a downward spiral.

We can find a new way to work with the inner child. We can embrace the energy of the inner child, listen to what it needs, and teach it a new way by providing it with comfort, support, and encouragement

Our task is to work with the inner child through prayer and meditation to re-connect it to the grace of God's love. Initially, the inner child is so traumatized by its experiences of pain, rejection, judgment, shame, fear and doubt that it is reluctant to come forward. It fears that coming forward for healing will yield nothing more than the same pain it has already experienced.

Just as you did in the previous chapter, use your safe inner space for the inner child to learn safety and security. When the inner child does emerge, you will be astounded by its wisdom, strength, creativity, vision and power.

Giving Your Inner Child Unconditional Love

Embracing your inner child is a repetitive exercise that enables it to recognize, trust and respond to the power of unconditional love. You build this trust gradually by repeatedly using your safe inner space with the inner child through meditations such as the inner child meditation from the previous chapter. Once you establish this trust, you teach the inner child a new truth, and you teach it to respond differently to its world. As a result, that part of you that has been wounded, demoralized, shamed and frightened emerges as the wise, loving and powerful part of your consciousness that accepts its ultimate lovability, worthiness, and ability to create and receive its good.

You can work with this process daily as a part of your daily time of contemplation. Begin by taking a childhood picture of yourself into your quiet, private meditation place and focusing on this picture while you chant the words:

I love myself completely and unconditionally.

If you do not have a picture of yourself, imagine yourself as a child. By focusing on this concept, you infuse your subconscious with unconditional love. At first, this may feel unfamiliar and even uncomfortable, because you are not accustomed to being bathed in unconditional love. Just as a prisoner who has been in solitary confinement has become so accustomed to the darkness that the light physically hurts his skin when he emerges, your inner child may initially subconsciously resist the light of love. You may find that judgments that you have held about yourself arise to counteract the words that you chant. You are teaching your inner child a new way, training it to respond differently, and this process benefits from patience and repetition.

Your Transformed Ego

By transforming these silent saboteurs, you can ensure that the coping strategies that you used to navigate during your formative years no longer sabotage your current desires. These are vital stages on your journey to prosperity. By embracing your inner child, you will hear the child's erroneous thoughts, and you can comfort the child, leading it out of confusion and into the confident clarity that comes from clear vision. You will redeploy the inner judge to seek its joy instead of avoiding the potential for pain. You will teach your inner critic to use unconditional loving acceptance to balance your inner saint and your inner sinner so that you live a more fulfilling life.

In transforming the silent saboteurs, you'll notice that they had emotional flare-ups that defied logic and reason. These reactions became habitual out of self-protection, because the memories of old scripts and the pain that these memories caused became an ingrained part of their routine behavior.

One way to heal the pain caused by emotional flare-ups of the silent saboteurs is to elaborate on the process that we've already used to work with the inner child. The next chapter provides another powerful exercise for doing this.

CHAPTER 9

SEVEN STEPS TO INNER PEACE

Healing is a seven-step process. Anytime your emotions flare up is a call for healing. When you have an emotional flare-up, refrain as best you can from expressing it in a way that can emotionally damage yourself or others. Instead, wait for an appropriate time to enter meditation and go into your safe inner space. As you meditate, you access answers and insights that can heal and transform your mind.

The Seven Step Healing Process

The following steps summarize the seven-step healing process, which I describe in more detail below and in my book, *Pathways to Inner Peace: Lifesaving Processes for Healing Heart, Mind and Soul*. The seven steps are:

Step 1—Acknowledge the emotion.

Step 2—Honor the emotion.

Step 3—Honor yourself.

Step 4—Express the emotion.

Step 5—Ask for the root cause of your distress.

Step 6—Pray for a miracle, and expect it.

Step 7—Rinse and repeat.

Let us begin.

Exercise: Begin the Seven Step Healing Process

I recommend that you read through this exercise before using it.

Step 1—Acknowledge the Emotion

The first thing we do when fear-based emotions flare up is simply be aware of them. Instead of suppressing an emotion, acknowledge it. You can acknowledge the emotion by saying something such as:

> *I am so angry, disappointed, sad, frustrated that he or*
> *she did or said this or that thing.*

Why you acknowledge the emotion

There may be many reasons that we deny the emotion. If we're sitting in a business meeting, it's probably not a good idea to stand up and choke someone, so we suppress the urge. We deny the emotion for many reasons, such as:

- We were told to.

- We believe that we should be in control. We shouldn't feel that way—I'm on a spiritual path, and therefore I shouldn't feel anger—I shouldn't feel pain—I shouldn't feel negation—I shouldn't have these feelings of inadequacy.

- Our subconscious programming says big boys don't cry, or if I am a woman and I rant and rave, that makes me a raving bitch. The need for the survival of the group which, as described earlier, is based on our vestigial pack-animal behaviors, causes us to discount the power and sacredness of our emotions because emotions were deemed to disrupt the group's overall harmony and, thus, threaten its survival.

Of course, there are times when it is inappropriate and unsafe to express the emotion. Find a private time and place where you can release the emotion and, at the same time or separately, enter your safe inner space where you can come to understand what triggered the emotion so the power of God's light can heal and transform the emotion.

Step 2—Honor the Emotion

We honor emotions by avoiding self-judgment for experiencing them. We recognize that this process is sacred and necessary. It is not profane. Optionally, you could even express gratitude that the emotion has arisen to make you aware of this opportunity and need to heal. For example, you could say something like:

> *Thank you for this anger, which has given me an opportunity to heal.*

Why you honor the emotion

Sadly, we've learned to dishonor our emotions. Many times, we discount our feelings, especially in a male-dominated society where emotions are seen as feminine. We feel a subconscious shame that compounds the negative impact that the emotion has on our subconscious, and thus on our lives. We don't realize that emotions are just signals.

> *Emotions are wonderful, divine tools that signal us when our thoughts and beliefs are not in alignment with the energy of love, and therefore do not bring us peace.*

As we understand our emotions, we can see them as wonderful tools that help us return to our natural state of prosperity. We can see our emotions as road signs that can move us back into alignment with the simple loving truth that creates our prosperity. Seeing our emotions in this way also helps us to see them more objectively, and to have a sense of humor about them.

113

Emotions are seen as something that spiritual people don't and shouldn't have. Emotions are also seen as these nasty, testy little things that cause disruption. Emotions are seen as disruptive because they have been misused. They are seen as damaging because when they are finally expressed, they are expressed in a torrent of destructiveness due to the sheer volume of emotion that has been suppressed for so long.

Imagine a pressure cooker, and the damage it causes when it explodes. The destructiveness is like a bomb. Therefore, learn to honor the emotion. Learn that if you are feeling pain, anger, or fear, there is a part of you that needs nurturing. All of you is good. All of you is acceptable. All of you is lovable, and the part of you experiencing an emotional flare-up is just a part of your subconscious that doesn't know it yet. This part of you appears so you can teach it a new way.

We honor our emotions through transformational prayer, meditation and emotional expression. In these ways, you can shine the light of God's unconditional love on the part of you that is experiencing an emotional flare-up. This lets it know that it is loved. Through prayer and meditation, you can give it what it needs. You transform this part of your subconscious so that, little by little, it reflects the truth and the light that it is. Through this process, every part of your being gets transformed into a gentle, loving, peaceful energy that has the capacity to attract and retain joy. Every part of your consciousness gets transformed into a reflection of the God Self that it is and that it was designed to be. We honor the emotion by being willing to see its role in our growth.

Step 3—Honor Yourself

Give yourself credit for having the will and the courage to examine the thoughts, beliefs and situations that have given you this opportunity to heal. For example, you might simply reach over your shoulder and give yourself a literal, physical pat on the back; or you could say or think something like:

> I am pleased with myself for wanting to examine why this situation has caused me to feel so angry (hurt, abandoned, unloved, etc.), and for my willingness to heal the part of myself that feels this way.

Why you honor yourself

Many times, we want to beat up on ourselves for having an emotion. For example, as stated above, *Big boys don't cry, so I must be a wimp.* Or, *if I'm a woman and I rage and scream and shout, and show my anger, then I'm a ranting, raving bitch.*

If we are already on a spiritual path and we have these emotions, we feel that we are bad people for having them, because we view the emotions as being bad. Therefore, we must come to the understanding that some situations are simply guideposts that show us when we have drifted away from the simple truth of God's unconditional love so that we can move back onto the pathway to prosperity. We do not judge ourselves for our situation, for it is a perfect opportunity to teach us when to align more closely to the consciousness of God.

Although we do not judge ourselves or the situation, we take responsibility for it because our thoughts and beliefs have created it. However, taking responsibility for something is not taking blame for it. Blame connotes that the event is somehow bad. This judgment need not apply to our situation because we have already established that it is the perfect opportunity to help us to grow. We did the best that we could when we created the situation based on what we knew then. Now that our consciousness is expanding, we know something different, and we apply this new knowledge to every part of our lives.

We don't punish ourselves for what was created out of the old knowledge because, at that time, we didn't know any better. Now that we know better, we have the power to change and to heal. We are showing great courage in this process of healing, so we honor ourselves instead of blaming ourselves.

Step 4—Express the Emotion

Expressing the emotion is the most important step in this process. As described below, there are many ways to express the emotion. For example, you can express with your mind, your voice, or physically.

Expressing with your voice or in other ways that can be loud, and perhaps alarming to others, is one of the reasons I suggested that you read this exercise before practicing it. In these cases, you might want to find a more private time and place so you can really put your heart into the expression. This can be done both during this exercise or separately, perhaps as a prelude to the exercise.

Why you express the emotion

When you express the emotion, you release old, stagnant energy that creates a void which is then filled by the light of God that you invoke by entering your safe inner space. This old energy is made up of repressed fear and anger that have attracted situations that give you opportunities to become aware of the emotions lurking in your subconscious mind.

For example, we may believe that we are unworthy of a partner who treats us lovingly. This belief may be stored deep in our subconscious due to past un-affirming experiences. This belief may create a frustrating new experience for us because we have been unable in the past to attract or retain a loving mate. This may make us angry at the world, ourselves, or the other person.

We express these emotions to make room for a more evolved view of ourselves that reflects God's unconditional love for us, the universe's unconditional support of all that we need, and our unconditional love for ourselves. As we express the old emotion, we move these old energies out of our subconscious so we no longer attract experiences that reflect our lack of love for ourselves. We then have more room for and attract a more loving experience.

Express with your mind

One of the many ways to release an emotion is with your mind. This is where visualization exercises come in handy. See, for example, the exercises *Emanating Light* and *Praying with a Snow Globe* in Chapter 14. In our safe inner space, where we have power, we can replay the situation that created the emotion, and re-experience the feelings. We can even visually fight our attackers and win.

We can also change the situation and its outcome. This releases the situation and its outcome from our mind along with any lasting scars that the situation has left, because we see the situation differently.

For example, at one point, I held an old, un-affirming memory of a schoolteacher who told me to sit down and shut up in an extremely forceful way. This memory was buried in my subconscious and made me feel like my contributions to any situation would not be valuable because I was not a valuable person. As a result, I didn't speak up in business meetings, and this arrested my career development. I went back and started visualizing myself talking back to the teacher, affirming my worth and affirming that my input had value. This transformed my subconscious from unloving to self-loving, and I regained confidence that I didn't know I had lost.

Express with your voice

You use your voice because much of the energy that we have suppressed has been suppressed in our vocal cords. In a private physical place where you are comfortable being loud, you can scream, you can cry, you can rage, you can beat your pillow. In the prior example, I used my physical voice to *tell the teacher off*. I also screamed and called her names.

Screaming, raging and cussing releases pent-up subconscious energy, and you will be surprised by the peace and the changes in your physical well-being that you feel as a result of this process.

If you have trouble beginning this process, you can start by using the sound *Om* as you think of situations that cause you emotional pain. *Om* is a Sanskrit word for God. When you use the sound *Om* with the intention of releasing emotional pain, the pain is automatically transformed because you invoke the light of God in the process.

Express physically

You can use your physical body because it holds so much energy. Our bodies imprint and store many of our memories. For example, when I was seven or eight years old, I received a severe beating. Almost thirty years later, when I had totally forgotten about this episode with my conscious mind, I was getting a massage and this memory flooded back into my conscious mind.

It was buried in the cells of my body (a phenomenon known as *cellular memory*) and the cells of my body had held that imprint until my subconscious was strong enough to release it.

Body work such as therapeutic massage, Reiki, Rolfing, energy work and energy healing can help us to identify those old pains when we are ready to release them. So, if you need help identifying these emotions and releasing them, therapeutic energy work can be very useful. You'll be surprised at the types of memories that flood in because, as you submit yourself to this body work, you are in a meditative state.

If you have difficulty releasing emotions physically using these methods, you can also use intense physical exercise. If you run, think of the anger, pain, rage or fear that you feel while engaging in a good run, and you will find that these emotions fuel your exercise in a new and interesting way. The exercise becomes more cathartic and you will be amazed at the amount of energy that you find. You can use other exercise such as swimming or exercise equipment such as the treadmill, the elliptical machine, the exercise bicycle, and the rowing machine.

Simply focus on the emotion, have the emotion and channel that energy into the effort. Physical exercise may be a very effective way to bring suppressed emotions to the forefront and, as with any activity, the more you do it the easier it becomes.

Frantically cleaning your house as a form of physical exercise can also be a good way to release pent-up emotions (and can be very productive as well). You'll be pleasantly surprised at how quickly you become comfortable working with your emotions physically. Soon, you'll be ready to work with your emotions in other ways in your safe inner space through prayer and meditation.

Other ways to express

Other ways that may work with emotional release are as unlimited as your creativity. In a secluded, private place, you can rant and rave. You can cuss someone out. You can scream, cry, or beat your pillow. Many people use drumming. Your powers of imagination are now expanded, and situations from the past or present are more easily addressed.

You have opened the way for unconditional love. A new-found peace replaces old grudges. Remember this tip:

When in doubt, cuss God out.

Step 5—Ask for the Root Cause of Your Distress

Ask:

What is this truly about?

What caused this?

Why have I created this painful situation?

You will become aware of the answer.

Why you ask for the root cause

We can create an unlimited number of situations that show us our thought patterns and where they are aligned or not aligned with the simple truth. Regardless of the situation, we will come to one or more of the following conclusions:

- I believed that God did not love me completely and unconditionally.

- I believed that the universe does not support me completely and unconditionally.

- I do not love myself completely and unconditionally.

Because these beliefs are not consistent with simple truths, we have had experiences that caused pain, suffering, fear, anger (which is fear turned outward), depression (which is anger turned inward) or deprivation. Our experiences are just as varied and unique as we are. However, the root causes of these situations are very uniform. These situations are not consistent with the following simple truths:

- God loves us completely and unconditionally.

- The universe supports us completely and unconditionally.

- We love ourselves completely and unconditionally.

Building on an earlier example, sitting in traffic is one of the most annoying aspects of urban and suburban life. You may ask yourself why traffic causes such a strong reaction that may range from mild irritation to potentially fatal road rage.

Your first response might be, *I am going to be late for work*. At a deep level, you may believe:

- You will be punished for being late, which is based on the misperception that there is a force outside of you, a surrogate for God that would punish you because, subconsciously, you believe that God punishes. This misperception is inconsistent with the truth that God loves you completely and unconditionally.

- Traffic always screws up your life, which reflects the misperception that the universe does not support you. This is inconsistent with the truth that the universe supports you completely and unconditionally.

- You deserve this inconvenience, which reflects a lack of love for yourself. The truth is that you have permission to love yourself completely and unconditionally.

Regardless of the outer situation, and emotions that are brought up as a result, the situation reflects a deeper misalignment with a simple truth. The situations that we create are merely guideposts to show us where we are or are not aligned with simple truths. Knowing this, it is easier for us to see all of our situations as tools of our own invention. These tools help us toward our ultimate goal of spiritual growth and development, so we can experience the bliss and peace that comes from realigning our thoughts and, thus, our experiences with the divine.

Step 6—Pray for a Miracle, and Expect to Receive It

When we become aware of the misperception that has created a difficult situation, we pray:

> *Mother-Father God, I have held a misperception in my mind. I have held energy regarding that misperception in my body. I have created difficult situations for myself based on this misperception. I have now released the energy created by this old perception, so I pray that you remove this old perception from my mind, my body and my affairs. I pray for a shift in my perception. I pray that this shift in my perception occurs so that I no longer create experiences based on that old and erroneous belief.*

Why we pray for a miracle

Before the New Age, we prayed for forgiveness of our sins. Now we understand:

> *Sins are simply thoughts or actions that attract painful situations because they are inconsistent with simple truths.*

Before the New Age, we learned that, *The wages of sin is death.* Now we understand that death does not come from a hateful, vengeful, punitive God. Death comes from beliefs that are not aligned with the truth. These *fatal thoughts* create situations that *kill off* our ability to experience ourselves as divine, innocent, loving, lovable children of God, because we kill off our ability to connect with the divine. Instead of a literal death, we die a figurative death.

As we gain a new understanding of sin, we understand that aligning our beliefs, thoughts and actions with the truth brings us peace, prosperity, comfort, joy, wholeness, and integration with our spiritual selves, our higher selves, and with more of God's energy. We pray for a release from erroneous, unproductive thinking. We pray for a shift, so that we no longer have those erroneous perceptions that cause us pain, grief, anger, fear, and rage. We pray for the perception that creates joy, love and harmony, and all that is good.

The miracle we pray for is a shift in our perception. We pray for the perception that God loves us, the universe supports us, and we love ourselves completely and unconditionally.

We also *expect* the miracle. Many times, when we pray we say the words, but we don't really believe them. Subconsciously, we still believe that God would withhold our desires. We affirm the words, but we don't really believe them. We still believe that the universe doesn't support our desires, or we believe that we don't deserve our desires because we don't love ourselves completely and unconditionally.

We may hold images from the past in our mind when what we wanted has not come to us. We may hold images where we have been frustrated, or where we have not been loved. We hold these images because that is what we know and can relate to.

Unfortunately, each past image and the imprint it leaves attracts the same thing to us, because we emit that vibration and attract its reflection. We have given the past power over us. Repeat the following affirmation over and over to release these self-imposed limitations:

The past has no power over me!

In our safe inner space, we can use the power and creativity that we have developed to envision and create new experiences. These new experiences are not based on the past. They are based on the glorious present and the glorious future that we create as the light of God shines on us in our prayerful and meditative inner space. We can pray that imprinting from the past be removed from our consciousness. In doing so, with expectation based on our new understandings, we create a shift in our perception that results in the miracle we pray for.

As mentioned earlier, if you play the lottery, yet every day after the numbers are drawn you say, *I knew I wasn't going to win,* you just waste your time and money because your expectation has influenced the outcome. The miracle we pray for is a shift in perception, not winning the lottery, but the example does make the point:

Expect a miracle!

Step 7—Rinse and Repeat.

You usually find the instructions *Rinse and Repeat* on shampoo bottles, and it encourages you to use more shampoo, much to the delight of Proctor & Gamble. In this case, you use this exercise as often as necessary to move you to a place of inner peace.

Why we rinse and repeat

Our experiences have often left such a lasting imprint on us that it is not possible to banish all un-affirming thoughts, actions and beliefs in one or two sessions. It has taken a long time to develop these un-affirming situations, and it may take time to dissolve them because they have become so deeply ingrained. Therefore, we repeatedly apply this process to all the un-affirming situations in our lives.

At first, this may seem difficult because our lives may seem to get more screwed up than they already are. This is because we have opened ourselves to a shift, and we are creating situations that give us the opportunity to see our erroneous beliefs and to heal them.

So, we repeatedly apply this process to anything in our lives that creates a situation that triggers us into an emotional flare-up, and we can create some doozies! As we repeatedly apply this process, we get better at applying it in the same way that we play the piano better when we practice our scales. The more we practice, the better we get.

Our consciousness is like an onion, and we have begun to peel back the layers. What we find is that our list of issues is not endless. It is simply a repetition of the same issues over and over in different situations. As we peel back more layers of a situation that triggers us into an emotional flare-up, the situations that we create become smaller to the point where eventually we create a lesson in such little things as finding a parking space, or a loving interaction with another individual as opposed to huge situations such as divorce, loss of a job, loss of a relationship, or loss of a loved one.

Rinse and Repeat!

In a Nutshell: Acknowledge, Express, Heal

A few years ago, I was talking with a friend who had a vague awareness of my profession, and he shared his view of my counseling. His words, though funny, were quite insightful, because they crystallized the misgivings that many of us have about doing inner work. He said, "Does this mean that I have to spend the next twenty years holding a baby doll, crying, and beating a pillow?"

I reassured him that he had a distorted view of what inner work involved. The energy of grace works much more efficiently than what he saw as a torturously tedious process of emotional angst. I told him that there are basically *three* steps to the process, that they can be internalized quite easily and used very efficiently, and the healing can be profound, effective, and very rewarding.

In short, when you are more familiar with the seven-step process, you can streamline it with the following three-steps to heal your silent saboteurs and remove any obstacles in your pathways to prosperity.

Exercise: Acknowledge, Express, Heal

1. *Acknowledge* the emotions that lie at the root of your beliefs, the stories that your subconscious mind has made up, and the experiences that those stories create.

2. *Express* (release) those emotions in a therapeutic environment where the healing energy of unconditional love can dissolve them. When they are dissolved, they no longer fester in your subconscious mind, creating the noxious experiences that you want to eliminate.

3. *Heal* these old energies, emotions, beliefs and stories by substituting the new truth that uses the law of attraction to draw you to your desires and your desires to you.

When used regularly, this process will become an integral part of your daily life and, eventually, in the time that it takes to inhale deeply and exhale, you will be able to change the dynamics of a situation so you can move forward with peace and confidence as you effortlessly create your desires.

CHAPTER 10

UNTYING GOD'S HANDS

Your heart is the engine that fuels your deepest desires.

If your image of a prosperous life is not aligned with your heart, it is less likely that you will have the motivation, focus, discipline or will to create the type of prosperity that you desire. For example, it is almost impossible to manifest a parking space in front of a destination if you don't want to be there.

To align with your heart's desires, you must know what they are. This chapter will help you become *heart smart*—that is, to become aware of the subtle, latent desires that have lived in the recesses of your heart, mind and soul. You may have dismissed these desires as outlandish, impossible or infeasible. You may not have made space in your practical world for these desires because they were inconsistent with what others needed you to be for their own gratification. You may not have seen a practical path for achieving these desires.

None of this matters. There is still time. There is still a way. There is still support for you, and you begin by identifying your heart's true desires.

Understanding Your Heart's Desires

Aligning with your heart's desires requires that you understand them. To become heart smart, ask yourself:

Why did I think I wanted what I already have?

When you understand *the need beneath the need* that your ego has already expressed, you can get to the root of what your heart truly longs to experience. The simplest way to understand your heart's desires is to remember this:

Ultimately, my heart wants to experience love.

We have developed outward images of what love means to us, and we are motivated to achieve or attract these outer symbols. We believe that if we have the outward symbols of the love that we seek, we will have the inner experience of love. Actually, the opposite is true. First, we must experience the love that is already within us before we can attract an outward reflection of it. We unwittingly set up a *paradox of conditional love*, when what we really want to experience is unconditional love. The paradox of conditional love puts the cart before the horse.

The Paradox of Conditional Love

The paradox of conditional love says that if we have the outward symbols of love, then we believe that we will experience the feeling of inner love that we seek. We forget that this feeling comes from within and must be activated within in order to attract its outer reflection. When we have not satisfied the outward condition that would tell us we are worthy of such love, we feel unworthy of this love. When we subconsciously feel unworthy of this love, we withhold it from ourselves and create self-sabotaging behaviors.

For example, I was once in a furniture store and noticed a mother whose son was buying her a furniture set. The mother, who was temporarily disabled and immobile, argued about the delivery date to the point that she unnecessarily delayed delivery of the furniture. Although humorous to observe, this *joy tax* was an example of the mother's subconscious inability to accept the gift that was given to her because of subconscious feelings of unworthiness.

Note: *joy tax*, also known as *guilt tax*, is a negative consequence we subconsciously draw to ourselves for daring to manifest our desires. Did you ever treat yourself to a new car and then lay something on the trunk and scratch the shiny new finish? That's *joy tax*.

I'm sure you can recall times in the past when you've exhibited similar self-sabotaging behavior. This inability to truly accept our good is so pervasive in sales situations that sales people are taught when they close a sale to accept the signed contract and say as little as possible to avoid saying *one sentence too many*, such as, "And by the time your widgets are delivered, we will have worked out the delivery problems and should be able to meet your delivery date." This one-sentence-too-many concept is commonly known as *talking past the close*.

I've also observed self-sabotaging behavior in dating situations, where plans are made and then a person says something like, "...unless you don't want to," which gives the potential date an option to change their mind.

When we engage in self-sabotaging behavior, it is often because we believe that we are unworthy of the love and support that we seek unless we have the outward symbols that our world has told us are representations of love. When we don't see these symbols, we subconsciously withhold love from ourselves because we feel unworthy of it. Instead, we can pursue the inner state of love so we can attract the outer reflection of that inner state; *this* is the consciousness of inner prosperity.

Getting Heart Smart Begins in Your Head

Most of the images of what we believe will make us happy are in our head, so that is an excellent place to begin understanding our conscious and subconscious motivations. For example, a pervasive idea in our culture says that everyone should be coupled by a certain age and, if that doesn't happen, there must be something wrong with us. This idea is typified by songs such as, *You're Nobody 'til Somebody Loves You*. We create an image of what our lives should look like, and then we subconsciously withhold our good from ourselves when our lives don't match the image. We forget that this standard of perfection is just a hallucination of perfection induced by an imperfect society.

This *should* image is stored in our heads and has nothing to do with our soul's plan, purpose or intentions. We work our way from our heads down to our hearts by understanding the heart-centered motivation that has bubbled up and formed the image in our heads. When we know the deeper longing that created our unique, head-centered symbols for love, we can move deeper during meditation and give the heart the love that it needs. This love heals the heart of any wounds that would otherwise block the creation of our symbols for love. This love that we send to our hearts unravels the paradox of conditional love so our hearts experience the unconditional love for which it has yearned. We then effortlessly create the outer symbols of this inner love.

We become heart smart by using the meditation skills that we have developed for more self-awareness. We use these skills to find out more about ourselves from the inside out. You've already had experience with this when you learned more about yourself by completing the *About Me #1* exercise and more about your conscious and subconscious desires by completing the *My Beliefs #1* exercise. In the meantime, you may have had a chance to expand or shift your consciousness based on the insights you have already gained from reading this book, so I suggest that you repeat these exercises now as you begin to develop a roadmap for creating your heart's desires.

Exercise: About Me #2

Once again, enter into meditation and ponder the questions raised in *About Me #1*. When you come out of your meditative state, write down the first thing that comes to mind in response to the statements in the exercise, regardless of what you wrote in the exercise *About Me #1*.

About Me

I feel best when I....

Time seems to stand still when I...

I feel joy when I...

Time seems to drag when I...

These are my loves...

These are my dislikes...

These are my passions...

These are my joys...

Now that you've had a chance to repeat this exercise, perhaps you can see differences from your earlier answers that reveal why self-awareness can benefit from practice. As stated earlier, repeat this exercise as often as you like and, when you're ready, move forward.

Exercise: About Me #2, with Reasons

About Me

I feel best when I...

because...

Time seems to stand still when I...

because...

I feel joy when I...

because...

Time seems to drag when I...

because...

These are my loves...

because...

These are my dislikes...

because...

These are my passions...

because...

These are my joys...

because...

Repeating these two exercises can be very powerful in helping you to determine your heart's desires. Once again, note where your desires are based on your heart's desires versus what others expect you to be or have expected you to be in the past.

Next, repeat the following exercise of self-awareness so you can understand and transform any beliefs that create experiences that you no longer wish to have.

Exercise: My Beliefs #2

As with the previous exercises, you will get the most out of this exercise when you begin by entering a state of relaxation. This exercise is also most helpful when you write down the first thing that pops into your mind, regardless of what you wrote in *My Beliefs #1*.

My Beliefs

At work I believe that...

I believe that my partner...

I believe that my body...

I believe that sex...

I believe that money...

I believe that power...

I believe that men...

I believe that women...

I believe that children...

I believe that I...

I believe that religion...

I believe that spirituality...

I believe that God...

I believe that my parents...

I believe that my friends...

Once again, each time you conduct this exercise your responses may vary. That could always be the case. As you continue doing the inner work of prosperity, your responses will become more hopeful and more affirming.

Laying the Groundwork

As you learn more about your hopes, dreams, joys, and beliefs, and as you learn why you love the things that you love, you acquire the vital information necessary to create your prosperity roadmap. At the end of the next chapter, you will complete a prosperity worksheet. This is the beginning of the roadmap that you will provide the universe so you can find your prosperity and it can find you. In Chapter 15 you will refine and complete this worksheet.

Be honest with yourself. In the same way that you give Publisher's Clearinghouse directions to your home so the *Prize Patrol* can find you, give the universe clear instructions so prosperity will show up at your door. This idea may seem quite radical to you, especially since we've been conditioned to believe that God (as a physical embodiment of the creative power of the universe) is capricious and gives to us according to His will, not ours. However, as we learned from the law of attraction, we can see the world as a mirror that reflects to us an external image of our subconscious so we can transform any part of our subconscious that does not expand the energy of love within us.

When we expand the reservoir of loving energy within us, we can then expand our experience of love in our outer world. When we see the universe in this way, it is a less capricious and random tormentor of our dreams, and is more of an impersonal reflection that changes as we change from within.

As we become aware of the internal confusion, conflicts and obstacles that keep us from manifesting our dreams, we can transform them so the bulk of our creative power can be focused on experiencing our good.

Untie God's Hands

As mentioned before, think of God as a physical embodiment of the creative power of the universe. One of the ways that we can put the full might of the universe's (God's) creative power into play in order to create our desires is by untying God's hands. We tie God's hands by being so specific about what we want that we actually thwart the universe's response by rejecting what does not match our very rigid specifications.

A woman I once worked with wanted to have a son. She specifically did not want a daughter because she remembered how much trouble she had caused her own mother, and she believed a daughter would cause just as much trouble for her. She was too specific by demanding a son, and became quite frustrated with her inability to conceive. The ticking of her biological clock had become ominously loud, and her frustration grew to a fever pitch. As I helped her work through her frustration, it became clear that what she really wanted was an opportunity to parent and to share with a child the unconditional love that she felt. When she realized this and removed the restriction that she had placed on the universe, she had a daughter within months, and within two years she had a son. It is amazing what can happen when we untie the universe's hands.

To untie God's hands, as you pray or meditate look at the inner state or experience that you want and remove any restrictions that you have put on it. Open your mind to all of the ways that a vastly powerful and creative universe can create an outer manifestation of this inner state or experience. And even if you have a clear picture of what you want, always end your request for this manifestation with the affirmation:

This, or something better

Untie God's Hands with Approximates

*An **approximate** is an outcome that contains the essence of what you want.*

In the previous story, the prospective mother wanted a child. The essence of what she wanted was to experience the feeling of unconditional love that comes from parenting.

I am reminded of the story of a woman who wanted since childhood to become a ballerina. She envisioned herself onstage performing and then receiving applause and accolades from an adoring audience. She had a tumultuous and chaotic home life, and the beauty, order, and serenity of the ballet was her escape. As her life progressed down a different path, she had children and aged until it was no longer feasible for her to become a ballerina, so she identified approximates. She used her professional expertise in marketing to support a local ballet troupe. Because of her expertise, the troupe became more successful. Her volunteer position became a paid position, and she eventually ran the troupe. As a result, she experienced the excitement, order and perfect choreography of ballet, and when the troupe completed a performance, she stepped onstage to receive the accolades she had always dreamed of with the ballet, but in a slightly different form, simply because she identified approximates and opened herself to them.

When you identify approximates, you send a signal to the universe that you are willing to let the universe support you in an infinite number of ways to bring you the *essence* of your desire, and you release your demand for your desire to come in a specific way. You may say, *I want to marry a truck driver who has a PhD* when, in essence, what you want is a mate who has a balanced combination of strength, intelligence and sensitivity.

To repeat myself in order to emphasize this important point, although many of the exercises that you will use are quite specific, including specific descriptions, pictures, etc., you can always release the universe to serve you most powerfully by ending your desire with the thought:

This, or something better.

Dark Times

In dark times, trust the infinite abundance of the universe and notice visual cues such as the seemingly infinite number of leaves on the trees that remind you of this abundance. In the depth of winter, trust that spring will come, and the magical abundance of nature will reappear. Even in dark times, the universe serves you with its abundance.

For example, when my mother lay dying of cancer in another state, I was despondent and depressed. I became so distraught that when I came home from work one afternoon, I unplugged the phone, entered meditation and went to my safe inner space, where I realized that it was my inner child who was so despondent and immersed in the terrifying prospect of losing his mother. I let my inner child express fear, grief and anger—yes, anger at God for taking my mother. As I felt the soothing, calming, loving energy of grace touching my deeply held wounds, I began to feel more peaceful about releasing my mother to the next stage of her soul's journey. I eventually reconnected the phone to find that I had seven (yes, seven) messages of kind, loving support from middle-aged women. These women symbolized to me the maternal energy of love that I was afraid of losing. The universe touched their hearts, literally working through them to send me the message that even though I was losing my mother, I would always experience the loving, maternal energy that my heart longed for.

Look Within

Our sacred task is to contact the love within us, which is and always has been connected to the great Source of all love. When we contact this inner, connected love, we activate the energy of prosperity that draws to us the essence of the prosperity that we have always wanted. Continually ask:

What is the need beneath this need?

We will find that the need beneath the need is always a form of love. We can even cut to the chase by simply asking:

How does love look and feel in this situation?

This brings us to the essence of our need. Then we can untie the universe's hands and let the universe serve us through the myriad of ways that God's grace can express.

This is a testament to the truth taught by Jesus when he said, "...seek ye first the kingdom of God... and all these things shall be added unto you," (Matthew 6:33) and when he described the kingdom of God, saying, "... the kingdom of God is within you," (Luke 17:21). He was referring to the profound, powerful love within you. When you connect to the love within you, you connect to the loving energy of the universe, and activate the powerful, magnetic force that draws you to the prosperity that you desire in your outer world as you simultaneously draw that prosperity to you.

CHAPTER 11

WHAT THE WORLD IS TELLING YOU

In preparation for your journey to prosperity, we will now identify possible obstacles that you might encounter along the way. You may think this means that your journey will be long and arduous, perhaps requiring years of therapy, but it is not. It is as simple as looking around you, seeing what you see and listening to what you hear. You can begin by asking yourself three questions:

> *What does my life tell me? (What are the recurring themes in my life?)*
>
> *What do my circumstances tell me?*
>
> *What do people tell me?*

We may think that we have a myriad of issues to resolve, but we really have only a few recurring themes. They have just metastasized over and over again due to the law of attraction, which keeps bringing them back to us and drawing us to them in different forms so we can have yet another chance to heal them at the deepest level possible.

For example, after years of hearing that it's not what you know but who you know, I believed I would not have the professional advantages that others had because I didn't have the right connections. This began manifesting at the beginning of my career when I received a job offer, only to have the location changed from Philadelphia to Cleveland to make room for the son of one of the company's executives, who wanted the slot in Philadelphia that had initially been offered to me. Several years later, another vice president's son received a promotion that I was vying for, and this pattern continued in one form or another for much of my career.

After deep reflection, I realized that this pattern and the feelings of unworthiness, hopelessness and rage that they triggered, stemmed from the ambiguous relationship that I had with my father, and the deeply ingrained belief that I would not have the advantages that others had because I did not have the benefits of a strong paternal presence. I believed that others would have advantages over me because they had the benefit of this strong parental force.

All of us have had similar recurring scripts. Here are some common ones.

I can't because my father didn't...

Subconsciously, we believe that our earthly father is a proxy for God, our Heavenly Father

What we believe about our earthly father is what we believe about our Heavenly Father.

If we believe that our earthly father is absent, unable or unwilling to supply our needs, or neglectful, we subconsciously believe that God is these things.

Our ego uses our spiritual creative energy to create an outward manifestation of our belief. As a result, we co-create the lack of support, encouragement, positive feedback, strong guidance and providence that we have expected from our father. We subconsciously support the creation of situations that make us feel unloved, unattended and unworthy, and this pattern feeds on itself until the anger, depression and rage of this energy crystallizes as a result of outer events that we have created.

Rarely do we associate these outer events with their real purpose, which is to provide us with an opportunity to look within to uncover the beliefs that have caused us pain so we can change those beliefs and align our thoughts with the truth of God's unconditional love. We often believe that if our father didn't do what he was supposed to do, we don't feel worthy of receiving our good. Subconsciously, we withhold our good until, eventually, we realize that an external experience can be an opportunity for us to discover and heal our ideas about God so we can co-create based on the truth of God's unconditional love instead of creating based on the illusion that God loves us and provides for us only if and as our earthly father did.

We can work with the inner child to re-connect it to the grace of God's love. As we teach our inner child of its perfection, beauty, lovability and worth, it feels deserving of loving circumstances and allows God's grace to transform it from being a silent saboteur to being a powerful, creative part of our prosperity consciousness.

I can't because of who I am

We often limit our ability to be happy and fulfilled based on our identities. On any given day, we may wear many labels. In our subconscious mind, we have given a meaning to each of these labels, and what we believe about these labels is what we're likely to experience.

For example, the label *single mother* may conjure up images of a harried, worried, economically deprived, guilt-ridden woman who lacks the support she needs to live a fulfilling and satisfying life. We imagine a person who is just one missed soccer practice away from losing her composure, and one auto repair away from a mental breakdown. In some way she may feel like a minority, as if she is a left-handed person in a right-handed world. She may associate a set of limiting experiences with being a minority, experiences such as professional discrimination, poor service and social discrimination. As a result, she may subconsciously support the creation of those experiences in the same way that my friend in an earlier example created drama in the grocery store.

Any label that we have assumed is an albatross around our neck, diminishing our experiences, can also be a catalyst for our growth and transcendence. When we work with meditation and self-awareness, we can discover a part of ourselves that transcends labels and the experiences that these labels create. This part of us knows no labels, no limits and no lack. It only knows of its divinity, its power, its grace, its beauty and its ability to transcend the limitations of our prior conditioning. When we tap into this part of ourselves and give it permission to dominate our conscious mind, and to overshadow the power that our labels have over us, we can create new experiences, and we no longer have to hold onto the limitations of our labels. For example, very few people see Oprah Winfrey, Condoleezza Rice or Michelle Obama as African-American women who suffer economic, social or professional discrimination, because their essence has transcended the limits of those labels.

This transcendence is not just for the historically oppressed. It is not just for women, racial minorities, gays, lesbians, and so on. Most people have felt left-handed in a right-handed world at some point or another, and have believed that these limitations have held them back from their true potential for good.

Your only label is Beloved; and, as Beloved, you deserve the benefits of your greatest good.

I can't because of who I was

We often feel bad for things that have happened in the past. We have all done things that we may not be proud of now. It is

145

important to know that we have always done the best we could with what we knew at the time.

When you let your past limit you, it's like trying to drive forward with your eyes glued to the rear-view mirror. You cannot make forward progress efficiently if your focus is on the past. You will become hypnotized by your past and repeat it, because that is what you hold in your subconscious.

Of course you can learn from your past, but when you pause to examine your past, look without staring.

I can't because prosperity is not of God

The paradox of perfection (that is, *I am imperfect, so I don't deserve my good*) and the guilt it creates, are deeply embedded in our subconscious minds. We have become so entranced by this idea that we believe that the way to earn God's grace is through a path of pain, suffering and overcoming challenges to prove our worthiness. As a result, we believe that an effortless, joyful, prosperous life is the antithesis of the path to God.

This idea has its roots in our DNA. As described earlier, when we were evolving as a species of pack animals, survival of the group overshadowed the importance of a single individual. As a result, we have believed at a deep subconscious level that it is noble to martyr and sacrifice ourselves in order for others to prosper. This subconscious belief has withheld us from our good, and it persists even though we have now overcome the environmental risks and physical dependencies that caused us to hunt in groups as pack animals. The vestiges of this subconscious belief have been encoded into our religious and social systems, and oppose our desire for prosperity.

In a prosperous life, we experience the grace of God that has always surrounded us. God has an investment in our prosperity.

146

When we are prosperous and at peace, we are shining examples of God's true promise. This energy emanates from us to others in the same way that a smile or a yawn causes another to smile or yawn, giving them subtle permission to shine as they are meant to shine.

I can't because it would be unfair (peer pressure)

We often subconsciously fear not living up to the standards of our peer group, parents, family situation or previously held notions of who we are. Our inner child holds this fear and resists our good. As we've mentioned before, once the inner child no longer seeks just the love of its immediate family, it looks to its peer group for the external affirmation that it needs.

The pressure to conform can be staggering, because the inner child believes that if it doesn't meet the standard it thinks that it should, it will not get what it needs to survive. In Japanese culture, a common saying for this is, *The nail that stands up gets pounded down.*

The adolescent group, an adult group, or the general population whose standard you don't meet may believe that your thinking is crazy, mind-boggling, witchcraft, or any of a number of characterizations.

But what is normal? Suffering is normal, pain is normal, lack is normal, conflict is normal, loneliness is normal. Are these the types of normal that we want, or that a loving and beneficent God would prescribe for us?

To move past the erroneous idea that we must conform to the standards of our peers, we can enter a self-reflective state such as meditation, where we access a larger portion of our conscious and subconscious mind. When we have entered this self-reflective state, we can ask:

> *When did I first begin to believe that I would suffer if I strayed from the expectations that others have of me?*

You can do this repeatedly, and you will see scenes of yourself at different stages of your life. Then you can expose these past experiences to the healing grace of God's unconditional love.

I can't because it's too much work

We believe that changing the way we see the world, ourselves, and our possibilities takes thousands of dollars of therapy, years of work, and our growth would stretch us beyond what is comfortable for us.

We *will* face truths about ourselves that we've been more comfortable ignoring or denying, and it is an ongoing journey, not something that will be resolved in sixty minutes like a television drama. However, the healing process will improve our lives each time we use it, and we will show results quickly and in a lasting way as we move forward on our journey to prosperity. Isn't this better than just repeating the same painful patterns over and over again?

Our silent saboteurs often mistake the routine of consistency for security. This idea has crystallized in the saying, *The devil that you know is better than the devil that you don't know.* We crave routine, even when it is a routine with negative consequences. We become addicted to routine because our inner child mistakenly thinks that routine is security, based on the belief that if it's fed routinely it will survive. This addiction to routine is why the potential benefits of making a change must be significantly higher than the negative consequences.

Routine is not security. It is a substitute for security.

Security, like any other quality, comes from within. When it does, we are able to feel secure no matter what is happening in our outer world. When we regularly comfort the inner child, exposing it to the unconditional love of God, we teach it that it is loved and secure no matter what is going on in the outer world. This process builds inner security. As we build this inner security, we become more ready to stretch beyond our comfort zone, because we know we will have what we need to survive, *come what may.*

I could if only he or she would...

Consciously or subconsciously, we might think something like the following dozens, even hundreds, of times a day:

> *I would feel better if only she would love me.*
>
> *I would feel better if he respected me.*
>
> *I would feel better if he agreed with me.*

Such erroneous ideas are based on the belief that our well-being is dependent on another person whose actions, thoughts, feelings, reactions or choices we cannot control. Each person has free will. Each person has *their* soul's purpose to fulfill, complete with the lessons that are theirs to learn and the experiences that they need for growth. This has nothing to do with us, and they don't owe us anything.

The radical idea that they don't owe us anything is the antithesis of all that we've learned. As previously mentioned, we have believed that our parents owed us more time, love, attention, respect, kindness, support, etc., than they could give based on their own experiences. We have transferred, and still do, this demand onto our peers, spouses, co-workers, friends and children, and in doing so we have placed our well-being at the mercy of others.

Imagine how much more empowered you would be if you no longer depended on others to feel worthy of your well-being. You would no longer subconsciously believe that you are a bad parent based on the actions of your child, or think that you are a bad lover because a prior lover made choices that had nothing to do with you. You would let yourself feel worthy of all the good that you desire, and experiences that you once saw as indictments against your inherent goodness, you would see simply as lessons to help you grow and heal. You would be ready to begin the journey into the world of your good by looking at what the world is telling you.

> **Note:** Although children and sometimes others are, in fact, dependent, and we are all interdependent, there is a difference between being interdependent and being *co-dependent*. The independence I stress is the freedom to be who you are and to attain the prosperity you seek without requiring someone else's approval or involvement.

I don't deserve prosperity because they were... they will...

It is a mistake to believe that God would withhold grace and prosperity from us because of the actions, behaviors and experiences of others in the past, or that the past must be a prologue to the future. These erroneous beliefs are created by our inner judge. The inner judge has catalogued all sorts of slights, and the pain that these slights have caused. It identifies strongly with its catalogue of slights.

> *The inner judge fears that its identity will be destroyed if the pain caused by its catalogue of slights is healed.*

The ego, in its role as the home of the inner judge and all of our other silent saboteurs, can be thought of as **E**dging **G**race **O**ut because it seeks to derail the grace that any challenging situation can generate. When we realize that this ego motivation keeps us in pain, we can transform any situation so the past is no longer the prologue to the future. Grace can change any situation, giving us the strength to respond differently.

Prosperity is for others, but not for me

We look at our heroes and believe that they have *something special*. The special something that they have is probably that they picked themselves up one more time than they have been knocked down. Their something special is that they didn't give up in the darkest of nights, because they truly believed that, "...weeping may endure for a night, but joy cometh in the morning" (Psalms 30:5). They didn't give up before their victory.

Our heroes' paths are theirs, and ours is ours. However, we have learned since childhood to compare ourselves to others as outward examples for well-being. If we fail to measure-up, we subconsciously judge, criticize and withhold blessings from ourselves. Subconsciously, we believe that we don't deserve our good because we don't measure up, and we don't deserve our blessings.

The erroneous idea that we don't deserve our good because we don't measure up is a manifestation of what a client of mine has labeled the *grinding guilt* that continually tells us that we are not good enough. Grinding guilt is healed as we expose to God's grace the erroneous idea that prosperity is for others; we do this through repeated meditation, prayer, and emotional release and healing.

These spiritual tools of meditation, prayer, and emotional release and healing transform the energy of guilt by exposing deeper and deeper layers of our subconscious to the grace of God. The message that this grace conveys is:

We are loved just as we are.

As we continually expose our feelings of guilt to God's grace, and feel the loving energy of grace, we begin to realize that this is not just a spiritual theory. It is a practical experience that transforms us at the deepest level.

Grinding guilt includes other erroneous ideas such as the following two beliefs that also sabotage our good.

I don't deserve prosperity because I was...

Our inner critic believes that God's grace and our good would be withheld from us because of our past experiences. Accept that, in any given moment, we did the best we could with what we knew at the time. We often forget this and blame ourselves for past experiences that make us feel unworthy of the grace that we desire. The subconscious dialogue is:

If that happened to me, then I don't deserve my good.

When we allow a past experience to block our prosperity, we fail to see its potential for actually helping us to feel worthy of our good. We assume that something bad happened to us because we've been bad. If we open our minds and release our preconceived notions, we can see that the experience was designed to show us that we subconsciously needed love.

We can give ourselves the love that we have longed for.

As we give ourselves love, more and more of our awareness is aligned with the unconditional universal love that draws our prosperity to us. For example, we may have experienced a lover who was unable to treat us with the loving respect that we desired. In this example, our inner critic is telling us, *I don't deserve loving respect because my subconscious believes that I'm not lovable.*

Instead of perpetuating this belief, we can see the experience as an outer reflection of an inner dialogue that tells us that we are now ready to heal. We heal as we apply love to our inner critic, which believed that we were unlovable, and we do not deserve our good.

I don't deserve prosperity because I did...

We believe that God's grace and our good would be withheld from us because of our past actions. We often judge past actions based on today's awareness. We know this when we find ourselves thinking:

How could I have been so....

Each experience is a lesson to be learned. Even an experience that we judge to be a wrong turn or an obstacle gives us another chance to shift our views and open to the Divine Source that is calling us to accept its embrace. Forgive yourself, and yet realize:

There is nothing to forgive.

What is the world telling you?

What are the beliefs that have created your life script?

- Is the world telling you that you are loved unconditionally, regardless of your past or current circumstances, or how someone treats you, or what you already possess?

- Where in your life do you need to know that the universe supports you completely and unconditionally?

- Where in your life do you need to know that God loves you completely and unconditionally?

THE SOUL OF PROSPERITY

- Where in your life do you need to know that you have permission to love yourself completely and unconditionally, and to accept love from others?

When your life is showing you something different from the truths in the answers to these questions, this is an obstacle to your prosperity, and it is a great place to start healing your heart, becoming heart smart, and building a foundation for prosperity based on unconditional love.

- What is the inner truth that you want to attain?

- What are some of the approximates that would show you an outer reflection of this inner truth?

The following worksheet will help you answer these questions in three areas (dimensions) where you wish to attain prosperity. Eventually, you can choose more than three areas but, to maintain focus, I recommend that you limit your initial choices to three areas.

Before you fill out the worksheet, the example worksheet can help you understand the types of descriptions you might enter. Later, you will build on this exercise to create your roadmap to prosperity.

Terms used in the worksheet are:

Prosperity Area # - Identify one of the three types of prosperity you are seeking; choose from: relationships, family, occupational, financial, physical, spiritual, or any other term as you see fit. This is one of the three destinations in your prosperity roadmap as you currently see it.

Clear, Concise Description - Using the present tense, provide a general, overall description of yourself and what you will experience when you have achieved prosperity in this area.

Physical State - Using the present tense, describe what your physical state will be like when you have achieved prosperity in this area.

Mental/Emotional State - Using the present tense, describe what your mental/emotional state will be like when you have achieved prosperity in this area.

Spiritual State - Using the present tense, describe what your spiritual state will be like when you have achieved prosperity in this area.

Example: My Prosperity Worksheet

Note that it is holy, right, just and good to include specific *things* in your worksheet even though, in this generic, personal prosperity worksheet there is minimal reference to specific things (e.g., a new romantic partner, a certain job title, etc.).

While things can be powerful symbols that trigger your creative process, things you specify are simply outgrowths of the inner state you wish to attain, and need not *tie God's hands.* Remember when you affirm specific things to add, *This, or something better.*

Prosperity Area 1 - Physical Prosperity

Clear, Concise Description - I am balanced, comfortable, healthy, vibrant and joyful. My movements, logistics and life circumstances are easy and effortless.

This takes the form of an easy, joyful and effortless commute, supportive life circumstances that are easy and convenient, and a healthy body that moves, processes food and thrives in ways in which I am comfortable.

THE SOUL OF PROSPERITY

- **Physical State** - My body is a conduit for joy. I am in physical balance, respond in a perfect way to physical exercise, and I am inspired to make affirming choices that support optimal health. I create life circumstances that enable me physical and logistical ease and comfort.

- **Mental/Emotional State** - I am mentally balanced, clear, and alert, and have a baseline experience of peace as I move through my world. Any emotional upset I experience is easily addressed in my daily spiritual practice, which returns me to a place of inner peace.

- **Spiritual State** - I am connected to the Source of all good, and this connection causes me to have a sense of well-being and inspires me to make the loving choices that create physical prosperity.

Prosperity Area 2 - Financial Prosperity

Clear, Concise Description - My financial situation is a source of peace and contentment, as my financial needs are easily met by the resources I generate with enough to spare and share.

This takes the form of an ever-expanding positive net worth, a car that brings me hassle-free joy and excitement, a home that is warm, welcoming and pleasing to the eyes and senses that I can maintain easily and effortlessly, enough money for exciting and fulfilling travel, and enough to share and spare in ways that bring me joy and magnify the joy we are all entitled to share.

- **Physical State** - My financial resources abundantly, effortlessly and joyfully allow financial expressions (home, car, hobbies and pursuits) that are sources of joy, comfort, peace and satisfaction, as an out-picturing of my inner state.

- **Mental/Emotional State** - I am at peace, which causes me to create and allow the financial peace I desire.

- **Spiritual State** - My connection with the Divine Source of all good guides my financial endeavors, decisions and desires to cause me to allow and attract the financial resources necessary for my joy, peace and fulfillment.

Prosperity Area 3 - Occupational Prosperity

Clear, Concise Description - As Florence Scovel Shinn, one of the mothers of modern metaphysics, said, "I have a perfect work in a perfect way; I give perfect service for perfect pay."

This takes the form of an occupation that allows God's good to flow through me and reflect my fulfillment, joy and peace unique to my soul's purpose. I am abundantly energized, supported and rewarded by my job.

- **Physical State** - Sunday evening (or prior to any service that I provide) is a time of joyful anticipation as I look forward to working.

- **Mental/Emotional State** - I am excited, energized and inspired by what I do.

- **Spiritual State** - I see the spiritual significance of all that I do, and feel the spiritual support of the Source of all good pouring through me to support those whose resources support me financially.

Now, use the worksheet below to choose three areas of your life where you want to experience more prosperity as you define it.

Exercise: My Prosperity Worksheet #1

To complete this worksheet:

1. Choose prosperity areas 1, 2, and 3 and write these in the worksheet.

2. Enter into meditation, where you can contact your heart, which is the deepest part of yourself. Focus on each of these areas, one by one, and ask your heart to tell you the physical, mental/emotional, and spiritual state that it wants to attain for each area. These are the inner states that will draw to you the outward prosperity that you desire.

3. When you come out of meditation, fill in the three states for each prosperity area. If the worksheet does not provide enough space, use another writing medium such as a spiral notebook.

Prosperity Area (Dimension) 1 -

Clear, Concise Description -

- **Physical State -**

- **Mental/Emotional State -**

- **Spiritual State -**

Prosperity Area 2 -

Clear, Concise Description -

- **Physical State -**

- **Mental/Emotional State -**

- **Spiritual State -**

Prosperity Area 3

Clear, Concise Description -

- **Physical State -**

- **Mental/Emotional State -**

- **Spiritual State -**

Don't be intimidated if the information you receive is initially unclear. You are still learning to listen to your heart instead of listening to those outside of you who have influenced you for most of your life. You can repeat this exercise as many times as you wish so that what you want to create becomes clearer.

As you repeat these exercises, remain open to the *still small voice* within you that would tell you of the many ways that you can attain the essence of your heart's desire. This still small voice is connected to the infinite wisdom of the universe, and it can thrill you with your creative power. Learn to listen, interpret, and act on the inspiration that you receive through this connection.

Exercise: My Prosperity Worksheet #1, with Approximates

Now, take the three areas that you have described with you into a meditative state and *wait* for internal inspiration on how to manifest the essence of these desires.

In addition to any changes or refinements to the prosperity areas that you have identified, you will receive at least three different **approximates**. These are ways that the essence of each desire can take form. For example, if your dream is to be a dancer, three approximates might be to work with a local dance company, work with a local theatre company, and produce a church play or dance recital.

The more you calm yourself, the easier these approximates will come, much in the same way as when you relax you can gather a thought that eludes you when you are stressed. Take all the time that you need. Remember that you might want to repeat this meditation exercise to be further inspired by the approximate forms that your good might take.

Prosperity Area 1 -

    Clear, Concise Description -

      • **Physical State -**

- **Mental/Emotional State -**

- **Spiritual State -**

My Approximates

-

-

-

Prosperity Area 2 -

Clear, Concise Description -

- **Physical State -**

- **Mental/Emotional State -**

- **Spiritual State -**

My Approximates

-

-

-

Prosperity Area 3 -

Clear, Concise Description -

- **Physical State -**

- **Mental/Emotional State -**

- **Spiritual State -**

My Approximates

-

-

-

The lion's share of creating your prosperity is the inner work. The great mystic Edgar Cayce said, "The mind is the architect of your experiences," and we've explored how your subconscious mind can either sabotage or support your desires.

You have connected with that inner yearning that you've always had. You have learned to open your mind to the many ways that your good can manifest, and you've become aware of some of the obstacles that no longer need to stand between you and your prosperity. Instead of relying on society's ideas about what your prosperity is, you have become heart smart by defining prosperity in terms that are unique to you.

Now that you have completed this exercise, and you know what your roadmap to prosperity will look like, you are ready to learn how you can you follow your roadmap as you move forward with creating your prosperity. We will begin by explaining the power of prayer. In Chapter 15 we will put the finishing touches on your roadmap and you can embark on your journey.

CHAPTER 12

THE POWER OF PRAYER

Prayer is one of the most powerful tools that you can use to create your prosperity, yet it is one of the least understood. Prayer is so powerful because it is so direct. Whereas in meditation we *listen* to the universe, in prayer, we directly command and mold the energy of the universe into the form that we desire. However, we rarely use the full extent of this power because, instead of commanding the universe, we beg it.

Imagine that you have a pet, and you beg the pet to listen to you instead of commanding it to listen. Just like pets, the universe responds with a reflection of your energy. When you beg, you are less likely to achieve the result that you want than when you command. When you send out the energy of doubt, uncertainty and fear, the universe reflects your uncertainty with an uncertain response.

When you command the universe with expectancy, you send out the energy of clarity, assurance and expectation, and the universe responds affirmatively to the certainty of your command. This truth creates a new type of prayer, the *affirmative prayer.*

The Affirmative Prayer

An affirmative prayer has four parts:

1. Invocation
2. Alignment
3. Affirmation
4. Thanksgiving

Invocation: Affirmative Prayer, Part 1

Invocation invokes the creative power of the universe by acknowledging that this power exists. By acknowledging the existence of this power, we become aware of it in a deeper way. Just as you begin to notice cars like yours when you buy a new car, when you acknowledge the existence of the creative power of the universe, you become more attuned to it. As a result, you draw more of it to you because energy flows where your attention goes. You feel this energy within you more powerfully as your internal experience of this power bonds with the outward reflections that it creates. That is why we often are stirred to the point of chills when we sing a powerful hymn such as, *How Great Thou Art*. We become aware of the powerful energy that we invoke. We can invoke this powerful energy in multiple ways. For example:

- By calling on God, reciting the many names of God. This enables us to tap into deep subconscious awareness of all the other people on the planet who have tapped into this energy.

- By stating the attributes of God that we want to experience.

- By reviewing the feelings that we get when we contemplate God.

Here is an example of one of the many ways that we can invoke an awareness of the presence of the powerful spiritual energy of God in prayer:

> *God, you are the divine Mother. God, you are the Divine Father. God, you are my ultimate provider. God, you are the comforter of my soul. You are my protector, God. You are the light of inspiration that I see around me and that I feel within me. God, you are the Source of all good, and*

all grace, and all peace and all joy. God, you are known
by many names—Abba, Adonai, Abba, Elohim, Jehovah. I
invoke all of the names that you are, and I unleash the
power of all those names. God, just the thought of you
fills me with the peace and comfort that I desire, and the
power of your grace is upon me now.

Wow. Did you feel a shift in your energy simply by reading those words? When you invoke the power and grace of God, it changes things immediately.

Invocation prepares you to create the energy, intention
and manifestation of your prayers.

Alignment: Affirmative Prayer, Part 2

When our energy is aligned with the mystical creative energy of the universe, the two energies work together and amplify the power of our intention. Once we invoke this great energy, we internalize it in the same way that we eat a meal after preparing it. In the song, *Pennies from Heaven*, we learn to turn our umbrellas upside down to collect the coins. We collect the spiritual fruit of our prayers by opening to a visceral experience of the spiritual energy that we have invoked. We align with this energy by using bridging statements such as:

God, you are the peace that I seek, and I am your beloved
child in whom you are so well pleased, so I open to
experience your peace as your divine gift to me.

God, you are the powerful creative force that created
heaven and earth, and I am your child, imbued with your
creative energy, so I open to experiencing my creative
power now.

God, you are the loving force that surrounds me and fills
me, so I open to experience a deeper sense of love now.

God, you are the infinite wisdom that finds a solution to any challenge, so I open to receive the flow of your wisdom now.

Alignment channels the sacred mystical energy of creation through your subconscious mind, aligning your creative energy with the creative energy of the Divine.

Affirmation: Affirmative Prayer, Part 3

Affirmations are universal truths or statements of fact that you would like to integrate into your being so they become your truth. The most operative part of any affirmative prayer is the affirmation.

To truly understand the power of affirmations, let's explore the power of a lie. When you tell a lie, by the tenth time you tell the lie, the lie becomes the truth. Of course, the first time you tell a lie, it is a lie. The second time you lie, the lie is still untrue. The third time you lie, you're feeling more confident because you've gotten away with it twice before, so you begin embellishing it. The fourth time you lie, you embellish it even more. By the fifth time, you've created a whole scenario around the lie, so it becomes a story. The sixth time, the story becomes stronger and stronger. By the seventh time, the story becomes cast in concrete in your mind. By the tenth time, the story has become so deeply embedded in your consciousness that it has become the truth. Your perception of reality has shifted, and you actually believe the story on some level. Because you have created the story with your words and your thoughts, it has actually taken form in your mind. The lie has become the truth.

If you can have this experience with a lie, you can have this experience with the truth of an affirmation. When you keep telling yourself the essential truth of an affirmation, this truth seeps more deeply into your mind and your energy. You begin to vibrate with this truth, and you attract its reflection based on the law of attraction. By understanding the power of affirmations, you can change your beliefs to align them with these simple truths of the universe:

- God loves you.
- The universe supports you.
- You can love yourself.

These simple truths enable you to create any type of prosperity that you desire, whether it be spiritual or physical prosperity, prosperity in relationships, finances, and so on.

Once we invoke the powerful sacred energy of the universe and align with it, we now hold the key to creation in our hands. It is as if this energy is divine Play-Doh and we can mold it with our words, our emotions, our intentions and our deeds. We have a tangible experience of God's creative power, and we feel and sense the divine substance of creation around us and from within us, so we use affirmations to mold this energy into form so we attract its reflection in our real world, and we become inspired to move toward that reflection. Instead of praying worriedly and plaintively to God to grant us wishes, we affirm our desire by claiming it. For example:

I now have the peace of mind, the clarity and wisdom to make the decision that is for my greatest good.

I now have the courage to take my next steps so I can move forward in a productive way in all of my pursuits.

I now have additional financial abundance with ever-increasing surplus.

I now have healing in my heart from old pain, and I am
open to the potential for new love.

Thanksgiving: Affirmative Prayer, Part 4

Once you have invoked the creative substance of the universe that is always in unlimited supply, integrated with this substance through alignment, and affirmed the form that this substance takes, you enter a state of thanksgiving. Just as a potter gives form to a lump of clay, your intention has given the divine energy a shape. You have co-created with the Source a new internal, energetic and magnetic imprint, and that inner magnetic image will be attracted to you. You will meet it half-way by moving forward in your outer world as a result of the law of inner cause and outer effect and the law of vibration (like attracts like). Some examples of thanksgiving are:

> *Thank you, God for the peace of mind, the clarity and the*
> *wisdom to make the decision that is for my greatest*
> *good.*

> *I thank you for the courage to take my next steps so that*
> *I can move forward in a productive way in all my*
> *pursuits.*

> *Thank you for additional financial abundance with*
> *ever-increasing surplus.*

> *Thank you, God for healing my heart from old pain so*
> *that I am open to the potential for new love.*

You can then release this prayer into the universe by using a phrase such as:

> *Let it be so, and so it is.*

Or:

> *Amen.*

In the remainder of this chapter, we discuss various ways to pray effectively that you can incorporate into your affirmative prayers.

Prayer is the key pathway to prosperity.

Affirm your worthiness, innocence and perfection

When you ***affirm your worthiness***, you affirm that you deserve your good. This truth drives out conscious or subconscious energies to the contrary. You overwhelm any subconscious feelings of unworthiness with the energy of worthiness that draws your good to you.

When you ***affirm your innocence***, you neutralize any conscious or subconscious guilt that would keep your good from you. We have often believed ourselves to be imperfect, and believed that our good is available to us only on the condition of our perfection. As a result, we have subconsciously withheld our good.

When you ***affirm your perfection,*** you eliminate any subconscious conditions that limit your ability to create your good.

Pray with expectancy

Just as a child performs up or down to our expectations, so does the universe. Pray with the expectation that what you pray for will occur, regardless of the obstacles that exist only in your mind.

With God, all things are possible.

Affirm your willingness

Sometimes, what stands between us and our desires is our own ego-based self, our fears, our habits that have become comfortable, our addiction to our victim mentality, or our doubt of God's love.

172

- Be willing to shift your subconscious so your prayers can be manifested in your outer world.

- Pray with the expectation that the inner change that you seek can create the outer desire that you want.

- Pray to release any conscious or subconscious will to deny yourself or punish yourself.

- Be willing to change yourself in order to change your world.

- Pray that your will aligns with God's will. Repeat over and over:

  My will and Thy will are one.

  My will and Thy will be done.

Your Personal Prayer Prescription

The secret ingredient in prayer is emotional release, which clears the emotional, energetic and creative space so your prayers can be effective. When prayer and emotional release are combined, prayer can effectively create the desires that you seek. Build your *personal prayer prescription* based on what you want to create in your world.

Prayer ignites the sacred fire that lives within you, attracting the infinite substance that you form into the energy that attracts your good to you in all parts of your life. Your task is to take this information and create a customized program of prayer, meditation and self-work to transform your life so you experience the prosperity that you desire.

The Energy of Prayer

When you pray and meditate, you begin to feel an energy. It may feel like a tingling. It may feel like an inner warmth. It may feel as if you are wrapped in a blanket of well-being. It may feel like pressure against the crown of your head or your chest. There are many ways that this energy can manifest.

This energy is the substance of creation. You can think of it as electromagnetic energy that attracts its reflection in the same way a magnet attracts metal shavings. Prayer works with this energy by directing it into the forms that the words represent. Prayer molds and refines this energy through the many ways that the prayer triggers emotions.

Praying with Emotional Energy

Emotions play a larger role in our creative process than we can begin to imagine. That is why it is very difficult to manifest a parking space for a place where you don't want to go. Your mind may desire it, but your heart does not. That is why we have spent so much time discovering our true heart's desires, aligning with those desires, and healing the parts of our consciousness that have not been vibrating with unconditional loving acceptance. The reason for this inner work of prosperity is so we can use the powerful, creative, emotional energy of love to create our desires most effortlessly.

Expanding Your Prayers

Prayer is not just the act of consciously praying. To get the most out of your prayers, expand your awareness of what prayer is so you use every prayer and every prayer technique as powerfully as possible to create your good.

As a reminder, every breath, thought, intention, emotion, word, deed, action and reaction sends energy to the universe, and the universe impartially reflects that energy back to you in the form of your experiences.

Everything you do is a prayer.

Chapter 13

PRAYING WITH WORDS

When we think of praying, we usually think of praying with words. As you will see in the next chapter, there are many other ways to pray. However, in this chapter you will see that there are also variations for praying with words that give your prayers power, and that you might not have considered.

Cadence and Rhythm

As you use your voice as an active part of your prayer process, you will find that your voice has certain natural cadences. For example, consider the beat of the Emily Dickinson poem, *I Never Saw a Moor*:

> *I never saw a moor,*
> *I never saw the sea,*
> *Yet know I how the heather looks,*
> *And what a wave must be.*
>
> *I never spoke with God,*
> *Nor visited in Heaven,*
> *Yet certain am I of the spot*
> *As if the chart were given.*

This is just an example, and you may find a different rhythm, but note how the poem begins with a cadence that is repeated throughout. Just like a drumbeat, this beat or vibrational rhythm sends out energy to the universe that raises your vibration. You become like a human drum, and the universe responds to your drumbeat. There is a natural rhythm within you that is consistent with your personal vibration.

As you find your cadence and flow with it, your creativity flows smoothly. You have seen the power of cadence and rhythm in action in many indigenous cultures, where the drumming, chanting sounds or other repetitive actions unleash a crescendo of energy to the universe. Perhaps you have seen modern derivations of this ancient energy in churches that use the rhythm and cadence of call and response to heighten the vibration and sense of connection of the participants. You have seen pastors who preach, or politicians who speak with a hypnotic cadence that draws listeners in. You can put this same power of rhythm and cadence to work for you in your prayers.

Praying with Song and Praise

As you find yourself getting worked up in the energy and power of your prayers, there are times when you may feel as if you are in an old Hollywood musical and can't help but break into song. This is perfectly natural because, as your vibratory rate escalates, it reaches its next natural level in song. That is why most church services are punctuated with group songs that raise the group energy.

Remember that the objective is to raise your vibratory rate and, thus, your personal magnetism, so you can draw your good to you more easily. So, if you want to punctuate your prayer or your inner work with songs, it is a wonderfully powerful way to send your energy to the universe and invite the universe's affirmative response.

You also raise your vibratory rate as you praise the universe for how it has already responded to your desires. Just as praising a child elicits more of the behavior that is praised, commending the universe invites more of the same reaction. That is why when you are thankful, you magnify the vibration of that for which you are thankful, drawing more of it to you.

You don't have to be shy about lavishing praise on the universe. The universe is not so neurotic that it needs constant affirmation, but *we* are so neurotic that we need to constantly remind ourselves that the universe does support us, because we often lose faith even in the face of overwhelming evidence to the contrary. By being in the vibration of thanksgiving, we continually draw more of what we are thankful for to us using the law of attraction.

Praying with Your Pen—Journaling

Many teenagers keep a diary as a way to record and become aware of their innermost emotions at a very dynamic time in their lives. As you move forward in creating your good, you are in your spiritual adolescence. It is an equally dynamic time, and journaling may be a powerful way for you to create change in your world.

Journaling is more than just recording your innermost thoughts. It is a way to commit the abstract ideas and desires to the creative process by capturing them on paper. As you capture ideas on paper, you begin to give them tangible form, moving them closer to physical manifestation.

One way to pray with the power of the pen is to write out and construct your prayers as part of a creative exercise. However, this is just the beginning of how journaling can move you forward in your journey to prosperity.

Journaling your emotions is a means of emotional expression. *Expression* means to press or move out from, so, when you journal your emotions, it is a form of emotional release. As you know from previous chapters, emotional release clears your energy of that which blocks your good so you can attract more of your good.

One way that journaling can help you clear your energy is to re-write your story. You can re-write your story so you are the hero or heroine. You are treated with respect, and you receive the support that you desire. You feel worthy.

Here is an example of how you can construct such a story. You can customize this story with the particulars of your life scene.

> *Imagine that you're walking from your childhood home through your neighborhood. As you walk down the street, you see a neighbor lady sitting on her porch. She is a wise, loving woman who exudes strength. You see wisdom in her face and kindness and compassion in her eyes. As you sit with her, snapping green beans, she shares her confidence in you and provides you with encouraging words. You are encouraged by her quiet strength. After visiting for a while, you know it is time to move on. As you leave you are startled by the strength with which she hugs you, which far exceeds what you expected from a small, frail woman.*
>
> *You move on, and see a broad-shouldered, middle-aged man mowing his lawn. He beckons you to come over, and he takes a break on his porch. As the two of you have a glass of lemonade, he shares stories of his past, and you realize that the strength that you seek is what he exhibits. He also listens to you intently. He listens to your hopes, dreams and aspirations, and encourages you as he*

acknowledges your abilities and your worthiness. He gives you a big bear hug, and you move along.

Next, you come across a group of children playing in the street. They are running, screaming, laughing and having a ball. They see you and surround you, singing Ring Around the Rosie, and you feel encircled with loving acceptance and you let yourself absorb their joy and your own as they continue their playful laughter.

You then proceed on your journey, taking in all the strength, guidance, nurturing, love and acceptance that you have needed for your journey. You walk a little taller. You believe that the world can be a loving, welcoming place at a deeper level of consciousness. You feel more assured, and you feel an energy of love surrounding you more constantly and more prominently than ever before.

In essence, you are re-writing your life script so that you receive the support, affirmation and love that you have always wanted to fill you with an inner confidence and sense of self-worth that will be out-pictured in your world in many forms of prosperity.

Praying with Others for Relationship Prosperity

As you know, your local television station sends out a signal. This signal is energy that is transmitted from the station, a satellite, or through a cable or fiber optic link and played on your television in the form of pictures. When you send out a prayer involving another person, you are sending out energy that activates the universe and is received by the other person on some level, largely subconsciously.

Many people have had the experience of thinking about someone intensely and then receiving a phone call from them.

179

This common experience is an example of the power of thoughts as energy that activates the universe. You can use the power of prayer with and for others in this same way. Although the person will always have free will, which will supersede the power of your prayers, prayer can be an effective way to heal relationships so you can experience more relationship prosperity.

The most powerful and liberating aspect of using the power of prayer with another is that the other person or people don't have to be present. For example, you may have a difficult co-worker, and her issues may impact your ability to enjoy your job experience. In a private, physical place where you won't harm yourself or others, you can release your emotions. You can also enter your safe inner space of prayer and meditation and imagine that she is sitting across from you. You can first release the anger, frustration and annoyance that you have with her, and pray that your heart and mind be healed of the misperceptions that you have carried about the situation.

You know that this situation has a lesson to teach you, and you just have not been able to move past the frustration of the situation to see the lesson and the opportunity for growth that is inherent in this drama. The fog of your confusion about this situation lifts when you let the power of grace lift the emotions from you that have clouded your vision. As we discussed earlier in the chapter, *What the World is Telling You,* this happens when you release the emotions and ask:

What is the truth for me to see in this situation?

Once you are filled with the loving grace that takes the place of the frustration and resentment that you have released, that grace brings with it a serenity and wisdom. You can ask:

Let me see this differently. Let me see the truth in this situation.

You ask this so you can see the situation from an entirely different perspective.

For example, at one point I had a co-worker who was extremely critical and negative. She seemed to delight in pointing out work flaws and difficulties, and she never seemed to be able to finish projects. Her attitude and her underperformance affected my work life, so I took her into my inner space of prayer and meditation. When I had released my frustration, the wisdom that filled that space gave me the sense that she had perfectionist parents who were withering in their criticism. I suddenly understood why she found it difficult to finish projects. If she didn't finish the project, she could avoid the pain of debilitating, soul-searing criticism. I also understood why she seemed so negative and critical. She learned it from her parents, and it was all that she knew. I realized that she reminded me of an aspect of my mother's personality in which nothing was ever enough. She also reminded me of a part of myself that felt unloved when my mother criticized things. Although my mother rarely criticized me, I lived in fear that someday I would be the recipient of her criticism.

With the grace that I felt from releasing the unloving energies that I had felt within, I saw the situation differently. I felt more loving toward my co-worker and was then able to pray for her with all my heart and soul. I was able to share the excess grace that I felt with her and pray for her as if she were there, because the process was really about opening me to more grace for my journey. My co-worker was simply a teacher, helping me to heal a part of my consciousness that she reflected, the part of me that doubted my abilities and feared criticism. As I repeatedly worked with her in this way, I began to notice changes in her behavior. She became softer, less critical, and more cooperative, and my work experience improved, creating more occupational and relationship prosperity.

This process works equally well for others who seem to stand between you and any aspect of your prosperity. One of the key relationships that may stand between us and our prosperity is our relationship with our families of origin. As we discovered before, we begin writing our life scripts based on what we observe and experience with our families of origin. We learn the rules of the road for navigating our lives based on these core experiences.

For example, I have worked with many clients who were taught that children should be seen and not heard, and this idea crystallized in their minds early in life because they were punished for speaking up. As a result of receiving punishment, the love that they felt they needed to survive was withheld from them. For many, this seemingly innocuous experience was seminal in causing them to believe that they were less valuable than others. Some of my clients carried this idea into pre-adolescence, and it was reinforced when they were mistreated or even violated by others and not believed or supported by their families, further diminishing their sense of self-worth. It is amazing how something as innocuous as a societal maxim designed to maintain order can have such a pernicious effect on the human consciousness and our ability to experience prosperity.

Often, we hold our families of origin responsible for experiences that shape our consciousness. To transform our consciousness so we can create more prosperity in all aspects of our lives, we must heal old family patterns, teachings that no longer serve us, and old family dynamics that diminish our sense of self-worth. For some, family therapy helps. For others, this is not feasible. However, praying with another, regardless of whether they are absent or present, can help to heal these family patterns.

For example, if the inner child is a girl who did not receive the affirmation, encouragement, support, attention and love that she needed from the father, her sense of self-worth may have been so diminished that she subconsciously chooses mates, actions and circumstances that are unsupportive. These subconscious choices are reflections of her seminal experience and the mistaken beliefs that these seminal experiences taught her—that she was not good enough, and did not deserve her good. As a result, the dream of even a simple degree of prosperity in any aspect of her life may seem remote.

Pat's Story

The following case study is a composite of many of the clients with whom I have worked. It demonstrates how we can use the power of prayer to heal and transform our consciousness in order to create more relationship prosperity.

Pat is a 44-year-old single woman whose father was an inattentive alcoholic. His inability to see his daughter's beauty early in her life caused her to feel subconsciously that something was wrong with her. Because her father was prone to violent outbursts, she always felt subconsciously that something bad was about to happen. She always expected the worst.

Of course, the universe consistently responded to her expectations, and she had lived through a series of bad relationships where her partners, just like her dad, could be alternately remote, volatile, or charming. Her sense of self was so diminished that she often gave much of herself in friendships, in work situations, and in life. Still, she didn't seem to be acknowledged or appreciated, partly because she also made herself invisible to avoid being the target of an angry outburst. As she approached her 45th birthday, she realized that she had become quite angry about her life situation, and angry at the world in general. She hid her anger with a façade of *niceness,* because that is how she had learned to cope.

Soon after we began our counseling relationship, it became apparent that Pat was angry at her father. She realized that, as an abusive alcoholic, her father would unexpectedly create chaos when he was drinking, and she had always felt off balance, waiting for the other shoe to drop. Because she was repeating the script that she had learned from her relationship with her father, she was attracted to men much like her father who were alternately volatile, remote or charming. She was still trying to get her father's love and attention, and withholding prosperity from herself with her subconscious script, *I cannot receive the love and attention that I desire; therefore, I do not deserve my good. There will always be chaos, and another shoe will always drop, so things will never turn out right for me.*

When Pat reviewed her relationship with her father, she realized that much of her anger at the world that she covered over had begun eating her alive in the form of various illnesses and physical limitations. Her physical condition was the result of dietary habits she developed to bring her physical comfort to compensate for her inner turmoil. She ate comfort food to bring short-term relief from her long-term pain in the same way that a lab rat ingests opiates even though these opiates will eventually kill it. She also realized that, because her father had passed away, and she had been conditioned to never speak ill of the dead, she did not dare to criticize her father.

Pat began bringing her father and all the subsequent substitutes for her father into her inner space of prayer and meditation. She began telling them how she felt, what she needed, and how their actions had affected her. She was able to contact and release emotions that she had suppressed. Then she was able to open this part of her to the loving energy of grace that had been blocked due to her hard feelings, which were actually contracted energy that blocked the natural flow of love. This unblocked loving energy was also able to touch, heal and empower her inner child, who had been so wounded, and the love began healing these wounds.

As Pat became more filled with loving energy, she experienced an overflow of this love, and saw things from a broader perspective. Once her inner child felt more complete, she became aware of her father's pain and the causes for it. Then she was able to have more compassion for him and, ultimately, she worked to release him and the power the relationship had over her. She was eventually able to work with the ultimate prayer of release:

> *I release you from any debt that I believed you owed me.*
>
> *I release myself from any debt that I believed I owed to you.*
>
> *I have enough love in my heart to let you be you, and to let me be me.*

We often hold someone—and often someone who is no longer alive—responsible for giving us what we need. We doubt that what we need is available from any other source, so we subconsciously withhold it from ourselves as we repeat the dynamics of that seminal relationship. This blocks our prosperity.

We build seething resentments, and deny our good and our prosperity as we contort ourselves to please others out of a fear that if they reject us, we will not have what we need to survive.

When we connect deeply and regularly with the energy of God's unconditional love, and realize in a deeply visceral way that is repeatedly demonstrated in our outer world, we truly believe that God is the Source of our good, and that God works through an infinite number of people, places and things to bring us our desires. As a result, we are less willing to hold others responsible for our good. As we feel the love of God working directly with us, we are less willing to betray, martyr or otherwise withhold from ourselves in order to gain love from others, because we are less likely to feel the need to earn what we already have.

As we moved through Pat's beliefs, emotions and habits, an amazing thing happened. In her safe inner space of prayer and meditation, she was able to identify, release and transform her anger. Through inner-child work, she was able to find the peace and comfort that she had always yearned to experience. She was also able to release the power that her experience with her father had over her to determine her well-being.

The psychic pain that Pat felt for so long became acclimated to the energy of unconditional love as she gave her pain a voice. The anger, rage and grief that had been locked in her subconscious became neutralized by the energy of love that lifted away the debilitating energy of anger. The part of Pat that had not felt loved, respected, seen, heard or valued became more confident. She developed a sense of worthiness, grace, wisdom and peace, and her outer world began to change.

Pat began to build better boundaries that made her more satisfied and less resentful. She began to feel more deserving of loving respect. She gained enough confidence to consider dating. Her professional performance and compensation increased as she began to ask for what she wanted. Overall, Pat moved forward significantly in creating the prosperity that for her, at one time, seemed to be only an unimaginable dream. With the repeated applications of the grace of God, where she had not believed loving grace to be present, Pat was able to turn her impossible dreams into a new reality.

Pat's Lesson

As we have learned, we often subconsciously base our beliefs about the universe and whether it supports us on what we learn in our early-life experiences. Then we carry this script forward and it repeats itself with others. Consequently, we then hold others responsible for our well-being, and we see them as the source of our well-being. However, we cannot control others, and they have never been the source. We can never control the lover who changes his mind, the friend who decides to betray us, the boss who devalues us or the child who disobeys us. They have been a reflection of our beliefs, so we can use the power of prayer to transform our beliefs and create a new experience for ourselves in which we are no longer willing to believe that our good is withheld from us, and we are no longer willing to block our blessings.

One aspect of praying to heal relationships is that these prayers actually heal *you*. Although you think you are praying for another person, these prayers heal you of any inner obstacles that are reflected to you based on your relationship with that person.

You may think you're praying for and about the other person, but you are really praying for yourself.

> *Every thought, action, deed or reaction is a prayer. It is your energy that influences the creative force that lives within you and shapes your world.*

You can use the power of prayer to support you in more innocuous life relationships as well. For example, prior to your next job interview you can imagine that you bring your prospective employer into your safe space of prayer and meditation. When you ask to see the truth of this situation, or how you can learn or grow from it, feelings of nervousness may come up for healing. You might then release these feelings and open to a new truth about yourself so you can face your interview with confidence. As you do this, don't be surprised if your potential interviewer suddenly becomes some other authority figure from your prior experiences. You can then heal that old energy so it does not follow you into the job interview and block the blessing of the new opportunity.

You can even try praying for another person as if you are on a date, and don't be surprised if the face of your imagined date morphs into the face of a different person from your past with whom you have unresolved issues.

No matter who you bring into your safe space, the process is the same as described more fully in the chapter, *Seven-Steps to Inner Peace*:

Identify the person and bring them into your circle of prayer.

1. Identify/acknowledge the emotional response that they trigger.

2. Honor yourself for having the emotion.

3. Honor the emotion.

4. Express/release the emotion.

5. Ask:

   - *What belief is creating this distress?*

   - *How can I see this differently?*

   - *What new information can replace the old information that caused this distress?*

6. Pray for transformation and release. Pray for a miracle, and expect it.

7. Rinse and repeat this exercise until the relationship no longer carries an emotional charge. Know that at some point, grace will take over and lift the long-held emotional charge from you.

Chapter 14

PRAYING WITH PICTURES

When you meditate, you open yourself to the Infinite Intelligence that pours its vision into your mind for your greatest good. Your mind then manufactures pictures that reflect the essence of your desires.

You can put these pictures to work for you in your prayers and in your prosperity self-work. You can find and post pictures that represent your desires on *vision boards* (also known as *dream boards*). Just like teenagers who post pictures of their heroes on their walls, you can post pictures that represent your desires onto large pieces of poster board. You can then stare at these pictures, embedding their images in your mind in the same way that an image gets burned into your computer screen when your screen saver doesn't work. As these images are embedded in your mind, you vibrate with them (the law of vibration) helping you to attract their physical reflections (the law of attraction).

For example, years ago I heard that BMW was developing a new two-seat roadster. I had seen some images of it and had already chosen my color, Montreal Blue. However, print images of the roadster were largely unavailable, so I put a four-seat BMW convertible of the same color on my vision board. Months later, when the car was finally released, I went to test drive it. My partner hated it. He was too large to fit into it comfortably and talked me out of buying it. I wound up buying a four-seat convertible in Montreal Blue instead, and although I was satisfied with my purchase, I was still somewhat surprised that I didn't manifest my desire for a two-seat roadster. When I referred to my vision board, I remembered that I had actually put an image of the four-seat convertible on the vision board even though I intended to manifest the two-seater. I was amazed at the power of a picture.

You can also use the power of pictures in your prayers. For example, when using affirmative prayer, use descriptive language that clearly, powerfully and sensuously defines your desire. Some call this *unleashing the power of poetry* in your prayers. The images, descriptions, analogies and metaphors that you use will increase your vibratory rate, increasing the power of attraction that you unleash from within you.

When you use visual images in your prayers, they trigger emotional energy that amplifies the result that you get from the universe in the same way that when you amplify your voice, you are likely to get a more pronounced reaction from someone who hears you. Note the difference between these two descriptions:

Thank you, God, for a new coat this winter.

vs:

I accept, receive and relish being swaddled and
comforted in a sumptuous new cashmere coat this
winter. I love feeling the soft, sensuous fabric against me,
and feel warm and nurtured in it, protected from the
elements as if the arms of God are around me, keeping
me safe and comforted regardless of what is going on in
my world. It is an outer manifestation of the comfort and
warmth that I feel as I am wrapped in the love of God. As
I place my wallet and cell phone in the soft, satin lining, I
know that the quality construction of this coat will
ensure that the deep inner pockets will keep my
belongings safe in the same way that God's love will keep
me safe. As I place my hands in the deep outer pockets,

191

my hands are pleased by the soft feel of the fabric, and I
am reminded of the rich providence of God.

Which of these descriptions triggers deep emotions within you? Hint: *swaddled* is a term used to describe the wrapping of a newborn (for example, swaddling clothes) that indicates a loving protection from the elements and shields the child's deep vulnerability from pain. This term alone triggers a sense of peace and comfort as well as an emotional release that unleashes emotional energy. The emotional energy that you release amplifies your prayer's effect on the universe.

Vision Boards

A vision board is simply a big piece of poster board that you use for pictures and writings. Catherine Ponder, in her groundbreaking work on prosperity, was a great advocate of vision boards. She called them *treasure maps*, but the intention is the same. Vision boards create pictures that reflect the essence of your desires so the energy of the pictures:

- Triggers your emotions.
- Elicits thanksgiving.
- Focuses your creative energy on attracting your desires to you.

Building Your Vision Board

You can build vision boards for many different purposes, but you always build them in the same way:

1. **Begin with a symbol** that depicts or triggers in your mind the power, loving grace and creative potential of God, or the universe.

2. **As your headline**, use a phrase that captures the essence of this grace in a way that is relevant to the desire you are depicting.

3. **As subheads**, you can use key affirmations, descriptions and phrases.

4. **Adorn the board with pictures** that depict the essence of the desire, and release it by adding the phrase, *This, or something better.*

5. **End each board** with a written expression of gratitude that begins with something like, *Thank you, God...*

Although vision boards trigger and fuel your prayers, they are much more than just input into your prayers. They are the beginnings of the divine alchemy that captures a thought and brings it into physical manifestation. You will find that these pictures have a subtle, magnetic power. You will be drawn to them, and they will be drawn to you. You will ultimately see physical reflections of these pictures in ways that will surprise you.

At one point, when I had a postage-stamp sized lawn that required only a push lawn mower, I was working to manifest a house that I had seen on my way to work. I imagined myself on the front lawn, which was about a half-acre, driving a red riding mower, and I put a picture of a red riding mower on my vision board. When I manifested the house and moved in, I was surprised to see a delivery truck pulling into my driveway and unloading a red riding mower. My mother, who had no clue about my vision board activities, had bought me a red riding mower as a housewarming present.

The energy that emanates between you and your vision boards animates those images, giving them life. That energy animates you, and the images in your subconscious mind attract their reflection in your external world.

One for the Money

One vision board can focus on your financial/economic situation. You might even choose to use green for this vision board. As with all vision boards, at the top, place a symbol for God, the Universal Flow of Good, or the Higher Power. You can also add a heading such as an affirmation from an inspired source that has emotional resonance for you and is relevant to the topic of the vision board. For example, "The Lord is my shepherd, I shall not want," or, "I will lift up mine eyes unto the hills, from whence cometh my help. My help cometh from the Lord, which made heaven and earth."

You can go to any game or party store and buy monopoly money, add extra zeros to the denominations and paste them on your board. For several years I used the IRS W-2 forms as well. I scratched out the current year, wrote in future years, and wrote my desired income in the top space for total income. Interestingly, each year when I did that, my income was within $1,000 of the amount I had written. You can use pictures that depict the financial stability that you desire, and you can write down your own affirmations such as, *I thank God for unlimited, joyful financial abundance in ever-increasing surplus.*

Although you may think you are working to manifest money, it is the need beneath the need that you want to manifest. You may think it is about money, but it may really be about the feeling of safety and security that comes from knowing that you are connected to an infinite source of sustenance that will meet all your needs and desires.

One for the Spirit

You can use a white poster board to depict your spiritual desires. Remember: "Seek ye first the kingdom of God" (which is heaven, and lies within you) "and all these things shall be added unto you." You can use affirmations that depict your innocence and union with God, such as:

> *I am God's beloved child in whom God is so well pleased.*

And:

> *I am loved, loveable and loving.*

It is often helpful to include a picture of yourself from childhood so the innocence and perfection of that child can be blessed and affirmed on the board.

You can list the qualities that depict how God sees you, such as:

> *I am innocent and perfect just as I am.*
>
> *I am filled with and operate with the unconditional love of God.*
>
> *I love and accept myself completely and unconditionally.*

By including these inner states of being on your vision board, you focus on these aspects of your inner self, and this inner energy transmits itself into your outer world, drawing its reflection to you. Its reflection is a more effortless, joyful and peaceful life because the fear, doubt, and unkindness of an unpleasant outer experience is neutralized by the grace of a new inner experience.

One for Love and Relationships

Your vision board for love or relationships can be hot pink, magenta or red to depict the passion and energy that you want to create in your relationship. You can include the essential experience that you would like to have in a love relationship. You can express the attributes of your potential partner, and you can include pictures of the types of potential partners that you feel drawn to.

When you list the attributes of the partner, and the attributes of the relationship, remember to untie God's hands by releasing these attributes with the phrase:

This, or something better.

You might also include affirmations that address any issues that have traditionally stood between you and the divine partnership that you desire, such as:

I trust the universe to bring my desire.

Or:

*I thank the universe that I am open to attract, attain,
retain, and sustain the loving relationship I desire.*

If childhood experiences, ideas or energies have been an issue for you, you might want to put a childhood picture here, too.

Occupational Expression

To quote again the agelessly appropriate affirmation for occupational prosperity that was originally coined by Florence Scovel Shinn, one of the mothers of modern metaphysics:

*I have a perfect work in a perfect way; I give perfect
service for perfect pay.*

You can use a thought form like this to headline your occupational vision board. Another that you can use:

God works through me, with me, and as me as I work.

It is very easy to use work as a proxy for your worth, and your work may trigger issues, insecurities, or doubts that stem from your childhood for you to heal in order to draw more prosperity to you.

Affirm your worth completely and unconditionally, and independent of your work, so your worth shows up in your work. Once again, remember that the mantra of inner prosperity, to slightly paraphrase the biblical verse, is:

Seek ye first the kingdom of heaven, and all else shall be added unto you.

When you develop feeling and energy patterns of unconditional worth from within, the results of your outer work will reflect your inner worth.

When you let your work determine your worth, you are putting the cart before the horse, because your inner worth determines how your worth is reflected to you in your work. There are times when you find yourself in a work experience that is vastly different from your soul's purpose, and you wonder:

How did I get here?

You got here just as the professor mentioned earlier got to the corner of the auditorium. In these cases, you can affirm that the path to your divine work is shown to you and you are supported and escorted by angels along this path in a way that is easy, effortless and joyful.

Praying with Active Pictures

There are many other ways that you can activate your mental pictures. You can imagine that you are a human projector and that a light emanates from your heart. This light is like the light that radiates from a movie projector onto a movie screen. You can see this *heart light* that projects clear, live, moving images of you and the state of being that you are creating. When you see this image, you can imagine how you feel in this state of being. As you experience your emotions, you empower and attract an outer reflection of this inner emotional state.

Note that while this prayer exercise is very similar to previous meditation exercises, the difference is that when you meditate you *listen to God* for instruction or information; when you pray, as you do in this exercise, you *directly command and mold the energy of the universe* into the form that you desire

Exercise: Emanating Light

Just as you do with meditations, sit comfortably in your chair, and begin by breathing deeply. By now, you are adept at concentrating from the exercises you practiced in previous chapters. Relax, and remove distractions from your mind and from your physical space so you can concentrate.

- Begin by breathing deeply...

- Inhale and exhale...

- Inhale and exhale...

- Inhale and exhale...

- Each time you inhale, imagine a golden-pink light flowing into the top of your head...

- Each time you inhale, you sense, see, and feel the golden-pink light...

- This golden-pink light flows into the top of your head each time you inhale...

- You feel this golden-pink light flowing into the top of your head each time you inhale...

- This golden-pink light flows down through your forehead and throat, and into your heart...

- Each time you inhale, this golden-pink light flows into your head and out of your heart...

- You inhale, and this golden-pink light flows into your head...

- You exhale, and this golden-pink light flows out of your heart...

- You inhale, and this golden-pink light flows into your head...

- You exhale, and this golden-pink light flows out of your heart...

- You inhale, and this golden-pink light flows into your head...

- You exhale, and this golden-pink light flows out of your heart...

- You see a movie screen or a flat-screen television in front of you...

- As this golden-pink light flows from your heart, this ray of light is projected onto the screen...

- At first the scene is hazy and unclear...

- You continue breathing the golden-pink light from your heart onto the screen...

- As you breathe the golden-pink light onto the screen, the picture becomes clearer and clearer...

- You begin to see a picture of what you are creating...

- You continue to breathe the golden-pink light onto the screen...

- As you continue breathing the golden-pink light onto the screen, the picture becomes even clearer as if it is now in high definition...

- You continue breathing the golden-pink light onto the screen...

- As you continue breathing the golden-pink light onto the screen, the picture becomes animated...

- You continue breathing the golden-pink light onto the screen...

- As you continue breathing the golden-pink light onto the screen, the picture become a scene ...

- You continue breathing the golden-pink light onto the screen...

- As you continue breathing the golden-pink light onto the screen, the scene repeats itself...

- You continue breathing the golden-pink light onto the screen...

- You see the scene happening again and again...

- You continue breathing golden-pink light onto the screen...

- As you continue breathing golden-pink light onto the screen, you become aware of how you feel when you observe yourself in this scene...

- You continue breathing golden-pink light onto the screen...

- As you continue breathing golden-pink light onto the screen, you give yourself permission to feel all your feelings...

- How does it feel to be in this scene?

- You continue breathing golden-pink light onto the screen...

- As you continue breathing golden-pink light onto the screen, you revel in your feelings...

- When you're ready, you come back to the here and now...

As you come back to the here and now, make a note of your emotional state while you were projecting the scene. Repeat this exercise (yes, you read that correctly; repeat this exercise, now or later) creating this emotional state over and over.

You are creating the emotional state of being in the energy of your creation. As you become more accustomed to this emotional state, emotional energy draws its reflection to you. The emotions are among the most powerful forces for creation at your disposal, and this exercise helps you to harness your emotional power to create your good. You can also use this exercise to change any situation that you currently experience by seeing the situation differently through your visualization.

Praying with a Snow Globe

A snow globe is typically a clear glass or plastic ball that has a scene depicted inside it. The globe is filled with liquid and when you shake it up, white flakes float around the enclosed scene.

You can place an image of a scene that you want to transform in an imaginary snow globe, then shake it up. When the snow has settled, you see a different scene of what you want to create.

Here is a prayer exercise to help you work with your snow globe to bring your pictures to life. As with the previous exercise, while this exercise is similar to meditation exercises where you *listen to God* for instruction or information, in this exercise you use pictures to *directly command and mold the energy of the universe* into the form that you desire.

Exercise: Praying with a Snow Globe

Just as you do with meditations, remove distractions from your physical space so you can concentrate. Then, sit comfortably in your chair, relax, and remove distractions from your mind.

- Begin by breathing deeply...

- Inhale and exhale...

- Breathe...

- Inhale and exhale...

- Breathe...

- Inhale and exhale...

- Imagine a golden-pink light flowing into your head with every inhale...

- With every inhale you sense, see, feel and become aware of a golden-pink light...

- This golden-pink light flows into the top of your head with every inhale...

- Feel this golden-pink light flowing into the top of your head with every inhale...

- This golden-pink light flows down through your forehead and throat, and to your heart...

- Each time you inhale, this golden-pink light flows into your head and out of your heart...

- Inhale, and this golden-pink light flows into your head...

- Exhale, and this golden-pink light flows out of your heart...

- Inhale, and this golden-pink light flows into your head...

- Exhale, and this golden-pink light flows out of your heart...

- Inhale, and this golden-pink light flows into your head...

- Exhale, and this golden-pink light flows out of your heart...

- Place your hands in front of your heart in a cupped prayer position...

- Let your fingertips and palms touch gently...

- As your hands are placed in prayer position in front of your heart, you sense energy flowing from your heart...

- The energy flows into your head when you inhale, and flows from your heart when you exhale...

- The energy flows into your head when you inhale, and flows from your heart when you exhale...

- This energy collects between your palms and your fingertips...

- This energy collects between your palms and your fingertips...

- As this energy collects between your palms and your fingertips, you feel this energy growing...

- As this energy collects between your palms and your fingertips, you feel this energy growing...

- As this energy flows from your head through your heart, it grows between your hands and forms a bubble that grows between your hands....

- This energy that flows from your head through your heart grows between your hands and forms a bubble that grows between your hands....

- This bubble begins to take the form of a snow globe…

- This bubble takes the form of a snow globe…

- You see the current situation that you want to transform in the snow globe…

- You see the current situation that you want to transform in the snow globe…

- You see the current situation that you want to transform in the snow globe…

- You shake the snow globe and white flakes float around the enclosed scene…

- White flakes float around the enclosed scene…

- As the white flakes settle, you begin to see a scene depicting your desire in the snow globe…

- You begin to see a scene depicting your desire in the snow globe…

- The scene depicting your desire becomes clearer and clearer…

- You feel as if you are in the snow globe, in the center of the scene…

- You hold this snow globe in your hands as it vibrates with creative energy

- You hold this snow globe in your hands as it vibrates with creative energy…

- You give thanks to the universe for the energy that has flowed through you…

- You now release this snow globe to the universe…

CHAPTER 15

YOUR PERSONAL PROSPERITY ROADMAP

In this chapter you will:

1. **Practice your prosperity worksheet** again to assess your current choices of prosperity destinations.

2. **Address any lingering fear, self-doubt, shame, or anger** that might hamper your progress. You do this through prayer, meditation, physical release, and communion with the divine energy that surrounds you and lives within you at all times.

3. **Revisit your chosen prosperity areas** to address any remaining issues. As a reminder, I suggest choosing three areas initially in order to maintain focus, but you can choose any or all of the following areas eventually, or identify areas of your own. The suggested areas to choose from are:

   - Relationship prosperity
   - Family prosperity
   - Occupational prosperity
   - Financial prosperity
   - Physical prosperity
   - Spiritual prosperity

4. **Complete your roadmap to prosperity**. Although you can always revise it and add new prosperity areas, this worksheet is your roadmap.

Exercise: My Prosperity Worksheet #2

Now that you understand how to create your good, you can customize your prosperity goals as you see fit. You already began much of this work in *Prosperity Worksheet #1* when you identified the key areas of your life where you want to enhance your prosperity.

Start by repeating the exercise. Enter a prayerful or meditative state and describe the physical, emotional and spiritual state that you would experience once you have manifested this prosperity. Then, you will receive a clear, concise description of a more prosperous life in the three areas that you want to enhance.

To clarify any issues that arise with the physical, mental, or spiritual state under consideration, you can ask the following questions:

What is the barrier that keeps me from this state?

What can I do to move past this barrier?

Use the methods that you have learned in previous chapters to address these issues (see the list of exercises at the front of the book).

Prosperity Area 1 -

    Clear, Concise Description -

      • **Physical State -**

- **Mental/Emotional State -**

- **Spiritual State -**

My Approximates

-

-

-

Prosperity Area 2 -

Clear, Concise Description -

- **Physical State -**

- **Mental/Emotional State -**

- **Spiritual State -**

My Approximates

-

-

-

Prosperity Area 3 -

Clear, Concise Description -

- **Physical State -**

- **Mental/Emotional State -**

- **Spiritual State -**

My Approximates

-

-

-

Address any issues that arise using the methods that you have learned in previous chapters. For example, in order to get this information to you:

- I had to heal myself of past shame so I would not be afraid of public exposure or topics that some might find controversial. I worked on this, and still do, because inner work is an ongoing process. I was fascinated by some of the images of shame that were burned into my consciousness, such as the shame of poverty that I felt when I was asked to go to the corner grocery store with food stamps. By continually comforting the part of my consciousness that experienced deep shame, I was able to release the fear that this debilitating shame would cause me more pain as this book, and what it reveals about me, became public.

- I had to heal my consciousness of any idea that, in order to serve, I must martyr myself and experience lack so I would resonate with the truth of this book on every level. Despite the success that I have experienced in life, I still subconsciously believed that it was sinful for me to be served so richly by the universe. I believed that I would only be loved by God if I sacrificed, martyred and withheld from myself. I had to accept the truth that God wants his children to prosper in order to allow my ministry to bless me in the form of this book that will bless many, including myself. This task included working to forgive myself for the many ways that I had learned to judge myself as unworthy of my blessings, and ultimately realizing that there was nothing to forgive. I regularly found, and still find myself becoming aware of reasons that my ego dredges up from memory that would tell me that I am unworthy of my good. I regularly have a spiritual flashback where I see myself as I was then, and I send the love of grace that I feel in the present to this prior version of myself, embracing my subconscious with the healing light of love so this prior version of myself feels worthy of my present and future good.

- I had to yield my ego's vision to God's vision. The clearest ongoing task for all of us is to yield our ego's vision of what our lives should be to God's vision of what our lives could be. My ego, which had judged me to be illegitimate, wanted this book to appeal to the broadest audience possible so I could be legitimized by proxy. However, the energy of these feelings sent the message to the universe that this book is not legitimate and it should not be published. This book was not placed in the right hands until I was able to release the erroneous belief that the book was not legitimate because it came from an illegitimate source. In order for this book to be deemed legitimate, my ego insisted that it be presented in certain ways to a certain audience. God had a better idea. Such is the case in all our lives. We must yield our vision to God's vision.

What You May Have to Do

Release any fear, self-doubt, shame, and anger that block you from your prosperity.

Replace these parts of your subconscious with the love that comes when you connect with the universal energy that many call God. Do this through prayer, meditation and release using the methods provided throughout the book. As new truth becomes the primary truth that lives within you, you increasingly project that truth into your external world and attract its reflection to you.

Release Fear—You may fear failure. The image of past disappointments may be so deeply embedded in your subconscious that there is no room for the image or energy of your success to anchor within you. The old energy that fears failure may hang on, preventing the energy of success from attracting its reflection in your outer world.

Subconsciously, your mind is asking, *What if I fail?*

Reprogram your mind to ask, *What if I succeed?*

211

Release Self-Doubt—Past experiences that were hurtful or demeaning may have caused you to doubt your abilities, your worthiness, or the universe's support for your endeavors. Because you are steeped in your un-affirming human consciousness, your mind is filled with doubt. Instead, through your prayers, meditations and communion with the divine energy that surrounds you and lives within you at all times, make your subconscious aware of love's presence. Then you experience *divine amnesia* and forget to doubt, judge, or withhold from yourself based on past experiences that create doubt.

Release Shame—You may subconsciously judge yourself based on your past, what you have done, what you haven't done, who you are or who you aren't. You may feel as if you have missed the mark and fallen short. As a result, you may feel unworthy of your good, and this feeling of unworthiness may have manifested in many ways throughout your life, compounding this feeling into a deeply held subconscious belief.

Remind your inner saint, your inner sinner, and perhaps your inner critic that you do not have to be perfect to be worthy of the grace of God. Remind them that, just as you are, you deserve heaven on earth.

Release Anger—Anger is fear turned outward. You can calm your anger by holding it in until you are in a private place, and then release it by expressing it loudly, drumming it away, beating a pillow, etc. You can also release it through physical exercise. Then, in prayer or meditation, you can search for the need beneath the need that leads you to the core need that can be healed with self-love.

All that you need comes from within you, because you create it.

212

God would not withhold anything from you. As you come to this new understanding, you no longer fear that something you need for your survival will elude you.

What are My Specific Obstacles?

You've identified the areas (dimensions) in your life where you'd like to enhance your prosperity. You've identified the approximates (the ways that you can experience the essence of what you desire). You have a general feel for the obstacles that are an endemic part of the human condition, and you suspect that some of these obstacles apply to you. Now you want to specifically identify personal obstacles and minimize them so you can create the prosperity that you want. In addition to identifying, silencing, and transforming your silent saboteurs, some likely obstacles are identified in Chapter 11, *What the World is Telling You.* When you have identified your remaining obstacles, you can apply the information that you've already absorbed from this book in a way that is most relevant to you.

Your outer experiences provide the most reliable barometer of your inner obstacles. What is your world telling you? When the world is telling you something you don't want to hear, it is easier to blame others. It is more convenient to project the problem onto your boss, your co-workers, your family, your parents or any other convenient person that deflects the creative power away from you. The truth is often inconvenient and unpalatable, so you judge that something is wrong and somebody must be at fault, and it *can't* be you.

When you have identified your obstacles, release your judgment that there is something wrong when a situation is one that you don't enjoy. Instead of judging the situation as being wrong, let yourself see it differently.

You can see the situation as an area where the benevolent universe is stretching you to grow into these loving truths:

God loves you.

The universe supports you.

You can love yourself.

*When you do not feel loved, supported or loving, the universe is offering you an opportunity to heal, transform and grow, and **this is your ultimate purpose on Earth.***

When you accept these truths, it is easier for you to accept that no one is to blame for any situation. It is part of the universe's grand plan, to which your soul agreed, to support you in the healing and evolution of your soul. It's not your fault. It's nobody's fault. It just is. When you release the need to blame and project, then you can take responsibility for the creative power that you have. You can realize:

Wow! If I created this mess, just imagine what I could create when I put my whole heart and mind into creating what I enjoy.

Own the creative power that comes with self-responsibility instead of wasting your precious energy blaming those around you for your situation.

Exercise: Identifying Your Obstacles

When you see this situation more objectively and without blame, ask your subconscious the simple questions that will give you clarity and transform your life. The key questions that you can ask yourself in most situations are:

How do I feel about this situation?

If I had to summarize the script that created it, what would that script be?

When was the first time that I felt this way?

If this feeling had to express itself, what would it say?

What did I believe as a result of this feeling?

What is the unmet need that this feeling evokes?

Is this belief loving to myself?

Does this belief reflect God's love for me?

Does this belief reflect the universe's unconditional support for me?

What is a new belief that would be consistent with my desire for this situation?

What is a new script that reflects what I desire for this situation?

What is a prayer of transformation that I can apply to this situation?

Working with the Different Prosperity Areas

Which three or more prosperity areas have you chosen, or have been revealed to you, as destinations for your journey? Use the following descriptions to help you address any remaining issues as you prepare for your journey.

Pathways to Occupational Prosperity

Are you having trouble with your boss, co-workers or subordinates? Your first reaction may be to move to a new job, but guess what? You take yourself with you wherever you go, and you will recreate the essence of the same situation with a different cast of characters. This is not to say that you should stay in a

THE SOUL OF PROSPERITY

miserable situation, but you can do the work on yourself so that when you move to the new situation, you leave your baggage behind.

Quite often, an occupational situation mirrors an old, unresolved family pattern. For example:

- Your boss may be your relentlessly critical father all over again, but this time in drag.

- Your co-worker may be your sibling, who always seemed to have your parents' favor.

- Your employee may act out just as your child at home does or like a younger sibling used to act out.

In many of these situations, by bringing people into your inner meditative space for release and forgiveness work, you can pave the way for more productive relationships. You can go into a reflective, meditative state and ask yourself the following questions.

If you don't feel affirmed, respected or supported, you can ask:

Where else have I not felt affirmed, respected or supported in my life or past experiences?

You can also ask:

What does this situation remind me of?

How does this situation make me feel?

When did I first feel this way?

What is the script that was created?

What is the new script that I want to create?

What is a prayer of transformation that I can use?

Do You Want a Promotion?

First, determine whether your desire is fueled by the unmet needs of the ego, or if it's the soul's deepest desire to express and expand. If it's ego, you are probably judging yourself and blaming yourself for missing a mark. As a result, you have moved into a subconscious spiral of withholding from yourself. If this is the case, you judge yourself for missing the mark, so you punish yourself by withholding from yourself, which creates more judgment. Your inner judge and inner critic are working overtime, so you calm them. As you calm them you are willing to let grace in, as only grace can reverse a subconscious spiral.

With grace:

1. You are willing to forgive yourself and open your heart to yourself and work with more unconditional loving acceptance.

2. You then allow the universe to support you in areas where you have subconsciously blocked the universe from supporting you because you didn't believe that you deserved the good that you desired.

3. This moves you from blaming yourself or others and opens you to the power and creativity and grace that lives within you at all times.

Are you blaming, or are you opening to creativity, power and grace?

Do You Know What You Want to Do?

If you don't know what you want to do, but what you are doing just doesn't feel right, you may find yourself in a position similar to the professor who allowed himself to be backed into a corner of the lecture hall. You may feel forced into one or more roles that are not yours but that you assumed based on your subconscious desire to please others or to do the right thing.

Your task is to get heart smart by claiming your innocence and identifying the approximates that would make your heart sing. Then you can move forward step-by-step to create the occupational expression that is more aligned with your heart's desires.

Pathways to Romantic Prosperity

It is almost a laughable cliché that if you want to create love, you have to love yourself. However, clichés become clichés because they are based in truth.

> *To create the love life that you want, first find that love within yourself.*

Often, we look to a partner to fulfill the unmet needs that our inner child still seeks. As we comfort, reassure, and retrain our inner child, we heal and vibrate with the unconditional loving acceptance that enables us to attract friends, family members and special others that reflect unconditional love to us in our external world.

Heal Your Inner Child for Romantic Prosperity

As your inner child feels more secure and trusts the universe, it trusts that it will attract the appropriate partner at the appropriate time and in the appropriate way. This releases anxiety and lack that thwart the creative process.

As your inner child begins to feel more secure, you feel more confident and peaceful, and this confidence emanates from you as an attractive energy.

As the wounds of the inner child are healed, you remember that at some level you have always felt beautiful, deserving and lovable, and you project this into your external world so prominently that it attracts its reflection just as a flame attracts a moth.

Perform an Exorcism for Romantic Prosperity

Often, we are haunted by the Ghosts of Relationships Past. We hold grudges against our prior lovers and, based on these past experiences. we hold beliefs about ourselves, about our world, and about our love lives. Then we project this energy forward into our next relationships.

In order to clear this old energy so the new energy that you desire can create the relationship that you desire, you can perform an exorcism (minus the pea soup and twisting head). In your prayerful meditative state, you can call forth all your significant past lovers. Which ones? You can tell which ones were significant by the emotional charge that you have when you call them forward. You can ask yourself the following questions:

What did I need from them?

Who did that need remind me of?

When did I first feel that I lacked what I needed?

How did this make me feel?

What do I need to express?

What do I need to know?

What do I need to hear?

What do I need to feel confident, whole and complete?

By asking yourself these questions in a meditative state, and listening to what comes up for you, you learn how to heal the wounds of prior relationships. You may find that your need was strikingly similar regardless of the relationship. You may find that the need that you identified and the script that you created around this need began somewhere in your childhood, and what you do comforts and supports your inner child.

Healing Family Patterns for Prosperity

We have learned about life, created scripts based on what we learned, held grudges, judged ourselves and judged the world based on our seminal family experiences. We often find it easy and convenient to blame family members for our experiences because it is easier for us to hold a grudge against them than it is to hold a mirror to ourselves.

As we move into adulthood, healing these old wounds becomes more difficult. We've developed the habit of blaming family, and this habit has become so ingrained that it is subconscious. Family members are rarely a part of our daily lives anymore; our parents may have died, and our siblings may not be nearby. We don't believe that we can heal these old wounds.

This couldn't be farther from the truth. This belief, and the family patterns that it protects, keep you from the prosperity that you say you desire. If your family members are not available to participate with you, that is not a show stopper. After all, it's not about them; it's about you. You don't need their presence to heal what lives within you. Your task is to attain a state of forgiveness so the old family patterns that stand between you and the prosperity that you desire will dissolve along with the old hurts and grudges.

Family Forgiveness Work

We think forgiveness is something that we do. Often, the beliefs, grudges, and patterns that reflect these beliefs are based on the erroneous idea that we didn't get what we needed from another family member.

To reword what was said previously:

> **Forgiveness** *is an inner state that fills us with what we*
> *used to think we needed from someone else.*

For example, perhaps when our father was absent or inattentive, we felt that we weren't worthy of attention—which is a proxy for love—and believed that we weren't attractive. We may have subtly held our father responsible for our feelings and projected into our world the belief that other men were equally inattentive or untrustworthy. We then, of course, attracted a reflection of this belief into our lives in the form of inattentive and untrustworthy men, and the grief, resentment and rage compounded itself, sending us into a subconscious spiral.

Initially, we subconsciously entered into a contract with our family members. We contracted that they would give us the love, attention, nurturing and respect that would support us. Often, due to their own experiences, they have been unable to do so. They did not know and learn unconditional love, so they were unable to give it. The contract we created stipulated that they owed us this unconditional love and all of its symbols, such as loving, respectful treatment. We then believed that they breached this contract and we held them in contempt as a result. Unfortunately, this contract only existed in our minds, and others were unaware of it. As a result, we hold resentments about slights large and small. We are holding them responsible, accountable and in contempt, yet they have moved on. We hurt ourselves, withhold from ourselves, judge ourselves and punish ourselves as a result, and we do this for no logical reason other than that we have decided in our minds that things should be a certain way, and others owe us something.

What we have needed is the love that comes directly from the Source. This is the love that we feel when we enter into prayer and meditation and feel the divine embrace. We have believed that this love must come through certain family members, and that these family members were the only source of this love. As we grew older, we transferred our demand for this love onto others, such as our peer groups, our lovers, and our spouses and children. Instead of holding them responsible for what we need to give to ourselves, we can open ourselves to the love from our Source. By doing so, we release others from expectations that they be what we need them to be for us, freeing them to be what they need to be for their highest good, growth and evolution.

We can release others from this unwritten contract by going into our safe inner space and feeling the driving influx of love that comes from the Source. As we open to this flow and experience the bliss and grace that result, we feel the internal essence of what we need and become more confident that the outward reflection of what we need will be drawn to us. When we feel the internal essence of what we need, we are less likely to hold those we cannot control responsible for providing it, and we can release them.

We can also release ourselves from being held hostage to their visions for us because of expectations that they have of us due to contracts that they have formed. This is a subtle, gradual process that is not always easy because our human ego thrives on these contracts and knows no other way to operate. We must work with this aspect of our consciousness regularly to free ourselves from the family patterns that may block our prosperity. This does not mean that we are eliminating family relationships. We are simply changing the subtle dynamics of our family relationships so that all can be free to prosper.

To heal these family patterns, bring the family members figuratively, not physically, into your prayer and meditation circle by using the methods already described. When you fill yourself with the light of grace that comes from the Source, and imagine they are also being filled with this light of grace, it becomes easy to work with the prayer of release:

As the Holy Spirit fills my heart with the love I need, I release you from any debt I believed you owed me. I have enough love in my heart to let you be you.

As the Holy Spirit fills my heart with the love that I need, I release myself from any debt I believe I owed you. I have enough love in my heart to let me be me.

Family Inner Child Work

An integral part of your prosperity work is likely to be work with your inner child. Each time, ask:

Where did I first learn the belief that now causes me such distress?

You are likely to see a scene from your earlier life and be drawn to heal that aspect of your consciousness. This often entails embracing that aspect of yourself, flooding it with the love that it has always needed, teaching it a new truth and a new script, and building trust step-by-step so that this aspect of you is safe, loved, protected, deserving and supported in every way.

Family Worthiness Work.

Often, aspects of your subconscious need to know that they deserve their good. As a result of internalized guilt, shame, and old scripting, they have felt undeserving. They have believed that they must be perfect in order to deserve the grace of God. They must be taught that, just as you are, you deserve heaven on earth.

These are the parts of your subconscious that we described earlier as the inner saint and inner sinner. The inner sinner believes that it has sinned and it must achieve sainthood in order to be welcomed into the grace of God and the heavenly peace that has been promised as a result of satisfying this condition. Teach unconditional love to your inner saint and inner sinner. As they become increasingly aware that you deserve heaven on earth just as you are, you will feel more deserving at your core, vibrate with this sense of self-worth, and attract prosperity to you.

All My Children

Caretakers have the most difficulty feeling worthy of prosperity. Often, caretakers such as mothers cannot control the actions of their children. Caretakers are largely unaware of the lessons that are a part of the child's life path and the sacred agreements that the child has made to have certain experiences in this life. This challenge is compounded as the media continually depicts parental perfection in the form of such characters as June and Ward Cleaver from the 1960's series, *Leave It to Beaver*. We have often believed that if our lives as parents weren't as idyllic as theirs, and if our challenges weren't as minor and resolvable, usually within thirty minutes, then we must be wrong and undeserving of our good.

When our children act out in imperfect ways, or the divorce, single parenthood, etc., of our parenting circumstances do not look like those on the old sitcoms that were seared into the subconscious of those in my generation, this triggers shame and an underlying feeling of unworthiness.

Our task is to see through the eyes of God that regardless of our circumstances, or the choices made by another that we could not control, we are still loved by God because God's love is not based on any outward condition.

God loves us simply for breathing.

This is the truth that we sear into our consciousness when we release the shame and guilt of the parent who cannot control the actions of her child. We go into prayer and meditation and we release these feelings that are not based on the truth of God's unconditional love, and we ask the Holy Spirit to take these feelings away with the transformative power of grace. By understanding how we arrived at our self-judgment that causes us to torment ourselves with the guilt of the parent, and by releasing this guilt, we open ourselves to the grace that would eliminate any obstacle to our prosperity caused by this guilt.

Healing Financial Schizophrenia

Our society fetishizes wealth, yet we have a deeply held spiritual belief that money is the root of all evil. As a result, as spiritual people we have a schizophrenic attitude toward money, and this often shows up in our financial lives. We have developed a belief that financial abundance is a proxy for our goodness. We have also developed a belief that to have money one must not be spiritual, and to be spiritual one must not have money.

Just as water takes different forms at different temperatures, yet its essence is the same, God's grace takes different forms, and one form is money. It is an objective medium of exchange, and any other meaning that we give it is just a distortion caused by the ego. When we pray to ask the Holy Spirit to release any judgments from our minds that would cause us to withhold our good in the form of money, we can clear this deeply held misunderstanding.

In our schizophrenic relationship with money, we believe that our prosperity is measured only in financial terms, because our society glorifies wealth. Comparing ourselves with more financially wealthy people gives the ego an excuse to beat us up and continue running the show of our lives instead of letting our higher nature create our good.

A wealthy person has a specific life path. You have a specific life path. Your path is not his, and his is not yours. There is no comparison. What God has for you is for you and will be revealed to you and given to you as you allow it to be drawn to you through the power of the higher nature of yourself.

The key to creating your financial prosperity is to understand why it is important to you. If you believe that financial prosperity is a proxy for your self-worth, then your task is to establish a feeling of worthiness regardless of your current financial experience, and then let that feeling of worthiness be reflected in your financial flows. If you believe that financial prosperity will alleviate pain and suffering that you are currently experiencing, then ask yourself:

What is my mind telling me that causes me such pain?

Often, your mind is not telling you that you are experiencing pain because of financial lack. That is generally a symptom. You are experiencing pain because of guilt. Your misplaced idea is that you should be something, someone or somewhere other than who, what or where you are, and you are punishing and withholding from yourself because of this guilt.

For example, if you are experiencing anxiety because you cannot pay your rent or mortgage, the pain may be because you feel shame about your situation, fear that you will suffer homelessness, and guilt because you have not met your obligations, perhaps due to decisions you have made in the past.

You find the source of this guilt by listening to the voice of your ego and all of its voices, such as the inner critic, the inner judge, etc. You listen to these aspects of your ego while you are in your meditative state, so you hear it against the backdrop of the truth, magnifying the insanity of the ego. You can then teach your ego a new way. Pray it into balance. Heal it with expression and release, and move more of your consciousness into the kingdom of heaven, which is the inner state of bliss that will then be reflected to you in your outer world.

Pathways to Physical and Spiritual Prosperity

Physical prosperity is a sense of well-being and physical comfort that brings you a sense of peace.

Physical prosperity is also logistical ease. Regular meditation reduces stress and its side effects and leaves you with a sense of well-being. Healthy exercise, of course, is also a great help in cases where it is possible.

Spiritual prosperity brings you a sense of inner peace, the peace that passes all understanding, and you feel a connection with something larger than yourself. Regular prayer and meditation bring you this sense of inner peace.

It Wasn't Your Fault

Did you know that every seven to ten years—except for the teeth, eyes, and brain—there is not one cell in your body that existed before (cells die off and new ones are generated). You could say that you are not the same person, yet you keep judging the you of yesterday by today's standards. The current you knows of its wholeness, its goodness, and its right to prosper. However, the current you keeps judging yourself as if you are the you of your past who experienced such terrible things and committed such terrible acts, at least in your ego's judgment. You keep judging yesterday's experience based on what you know today. Yesterday, you didn't know the truth. Yesterday, you hadn't applied the truth. Yesterday, you hadn't found a new way and neither had those around you. You can't judge yourself, your experience or your circumstances of yesterday by today's standards.

It wasn't your fault.

Drum this message into your consciousness layer by layer. This is why the process of healing and growth that results in prosperity is a repetitive process. Be patient with yourself, because you are healing your deeply held consciousness. Just as it takes patience and repetition to train an animal, it takes patience and repetition to transform the intransigent aspects of your *ego consciousness*. It takes time to soothe and nurture your inner child so it can trust. It takes time to redeploy your inner judge and to focus your inner critic on productive pursuits.

What occurs in your outer world is in keeping with the universe's loving conspiracy to heal your soul. The universe will always present you with the experiences, information and situations designed to let you see an outer reflection of your subconscious so you can heal the obstacles to your prosperity. Your task is simply to stop, look and listen.

- You stop when you meditate.

- You look when you release judgment so that you unflinchingly see the truth that your ego does not want you to see.

- You listen to this truth, transforming the misperceptions that have clouded your mind.

When you judge yourself or your situations, you simply stand in the way of the universe, interfering with its ability to heal your soul and deliver to you the prosperity that is your birthright.

The most common obstacle to our good is guilt caused by past experiences.

Completing Your Prosperity Roadmap

Congratulations! Now, it is time to create your personal prosperity plan. Your personal prosperity plan:

- Identifies the areas of your life where you want to experience more prosperity.

- Identifies issues in those areas that keep you from your prosperity.

- Applies the tools that will heal and shift your consciousness to these areas so you can create the prosperity that you desire.

The good news is that you've already done it. Now you just apply it in a consistent way, considering the repetitive nature of personal growth.

Exercise: My Prosperity Worksheet #3

You are ready to put the finishing touches on your roadmap to prosperity. Begin by elaborating on the prosperity worksheet that you completed earlier and revisited at the beginning of this chapter, this time elaborating on the self-work that you will employ to create your prosperity.

Note that I have added *intermediate steps*. These give you an opportunity to assess your progress and see if you need to modify your vision or how you approach your vision.

229

These intermediate steps are often the practical tasks that must be completed to facilitate your prosperity. For example, in order to get a new job, you may have to update your resume, distribute it and, when you have interviews, follow-up with your interviewers.

As you complete this worksheet again, you may find yourself revising or correcting and adding to your previous responses. These corrections will often happen because of new information or new insights that you receive, and because the process of creating your good is a dynamic process that is infused with the infinite creativity of God's grace. Be flexible, and be patient with yourself.

Prosperity Area 1 -

- **Clear, Concise Description –**

- **Physical State -**

- **Mental/Emotional State -**

- **Spiritual State -**

My Approximates

-
-
-

- What blocks me from this blessing?

- Which unproductive beliefs?

- Which unproductive aspects of my ego consciousness? (e.g., inner judge, inner child, inner critic, etc.)

- Where did I learn this?

- What is the new truth?

- Which tools can I use to adopt this new truth in the deepest levels of my consciousness? (e.g., healing the inner child, healing old family wounds, bringing people into my safe inner space, emotional release of old shame or guilt, etc.)

- What are my next steps? (e.g., create a vision board and meditate on it, apply for the new position I've been afraid to apply for, etc.)

- What are my intermediate steps? (e.g., to get a new job, intermediate steps might be to update your resume, distribute it, and follow-up with interviewers.)

- What is the ultimate vision that has appeared in my mind based on new information?

Prosperity Area 2 -

Clear, Concise Description -

- **Physical State -**

- **Mental/Emotional State -**

- **Spiritual State -**

My Approximates

-

-

-

- What blocks me from this blessing?

- Which unproductive beliefs?

- Which unproductive aspects of my ego consciousness?
  (e.g., inner judge, inner child, inner critic, etc.)

- Where did I learn this?

- What is the new truth?

- Which tools can I use to adopt this new truth in the deepest levels of my consciousness? (e.g., healing the inner child, healing old family wounds, bringing people into my safe inner space, emotional release of old shame or guilt, etc.)

- What are my next steps? (e.g., create a vision board and meditate on it, apply for the new position I've been afraid to apply for, etc.)

- What are my intermediate steps? (e.g., to get a new job, intermediate steps might be to update your resume, distribute it, and follow-up with interviewers.)

- What is the ultimate vision that has appeared in my mind based on new information?

Prosperity Area 3 -

Clear, Concise Description -

- **Physical State -**

- **Mental/Emotional State -**

- **Spiritual State -**

My Approximates

-

-

-

- What blocks me from this blessing?

- Which unproductive beliefs?

- Which unproductive aspects of my ego consciousness? (e.g., inner judge, inner child, inner critic, etc.)

- Where did I learn this?

- What is the new truth?

- Which tools can I use to adopt this new truth in the deepest levels of my consciousness? (e.g., healing the inner child, healing old family wounds, bringing people into my safe inner space, emotional release of old shame or guilt, etc.)

- What are my next steps? (e.g., create a vision board and meditate on it, apply for the new position I've been afraid to apply for, etc.)

- What are my intermediate steps? (e.g., to get a new job, intermediate steps might be to update your resume, distribute it, and follow-up with interviewers.)

- What is the ultimate vision that has appeared in my mind based on new information?

When you have completed this exercise, you have a clear roadmap of all that you do to create prosperity in any and every area of your life.

CHAPTER 16

RINSE AND REPEAT

Just as old friends have difficulty saying goodbye, and linger with just *one more* one-more thought, this final chapter discusses several other things that are helpful to know as you take your journey. By way of beginning to say goodbye, let me remind you of words you have heard many times, and I hope you take to heart:

If at first you don't succeed, *try, try again.*

We are building a new consciousness of prosperity, moment by moment and day by day. It is extensive work and it doesn't happen overnight. In fact, even after you reach your prosperity goals, it is likely that you will recognize the benefits of prayer, meditation, and emotional release and these will become an integral part of your life.

Our consciousness has formed and crystallized over a period of decades, and transforming it is a repetitive process that won't take decades, but it will take more than a few seconds. This is where patience with yourself and compassion for yourself are important. You can begin to have this patience and compassion as you understand why the power of repetition is so important in creating the prosperity you desire.

Let's look at how any habit is formed. When you learn to hit a baseball, you first learn how to hold the bat. Then you learn how to swing the bat, concentrate on the ball, and coordinate your swing so it coincides with the arrival and position of the ball. When you swing and miss, you call it a strike, but a strike can be very valuable. Each time you hit or miss the ball, your brain collects information on how to hold the bat, position the bat, swing the bat and hit the ball based on the velocity and trajectory of the ball. The brain uses this data to sharpen its calculation on how to time the swing to get a hit, and even a home run. With each swing, the calculations become a bit more exact. Eventually, professional baseball players don't think about how to hit the ball. Their eyes, arms, muscles and brains work together to perform complex calculations on how and when to hit the ball based on the ball's velocity and trajectory. The baseball player has integrated this knowledge so deeply that it becomes a reflex.

Just as a baseball player integrates information, you have integrated former, erroneous information so deeply that it is your default state, and it takes a conscious commitment to become aware of all the ways that you integrated the old, erroneous information. This becomes especially difficult because evidence of the old, erroneous information is pervasive in your subconscious. This evidence has created some degree of pain and suffering, so it has imprinted in your mind much more prominently than the image of the new information and the outcomes that the new truth can bring. Actually, some scientists have noted that the potential positive outcome of a new choice has to almost double the existing negative consequences of an existing choice in order for a person to make a change.

You Will Encounter Obstacles

Expect that you will encounter obstacles, and don't judge yourself when you do. At most, simply say:

Oops, I did it again.

Or:

I thought I dealt with that.

Obstacles are good things. Just as every swing gives the baseball player important data, every obstacle gives you data on your

239

thoughts, actions and reactions that reflect and reinforce either the past belief that has been painful for you or the new belief that you want to adopt and manifest.

Your mind has been conditioned to believe that if you encounter obstacles, you have done something wrong. Actually, you have done something right. When you encounter an obstacle, you have moved forward, and the light has moved deeper into your subconscious.

> *Obstacles don't indicate your lack of progress. They*
> *indicate your progress.*

You are peeling back your consciousness, layer by layer, and you just discovered a new layer. In time, you will become so adept at working your process of prayer, meditation and release that you will not become frustrated when you have to review the same material again. You will remove judgment of yourself so completely that you will be at peace no matter what. Just as Babe Ruth led major league baseball in both home runs and strikeouts several times, obstacles inspire new growth and healing deep within your subconscious.

Believe in Your Progress

We have been conditioned to believe that humility is a virtue, and to downplay even the smallest successes.

> *Humility is highly overrated.*

We have also been conditioned to believe that the Lord giveth and the Lord taketh away. We subconsciously fear that our progress will be temporary at best, and we dare not risk jinxing it by celebrating. Our minds are conditioned to believe that we always have farther to go.

This conditioning is based on the erroneous idea that we have always fallen short of God's grace. As a result of this skewed perception, we may have traveled ninety-nine yards toward a touchdown and have only one more yard to go, but we believe that final yard is just as daunting as the first ninety-nine.

We can overcome this perception with practice, and it is worthwhile to celebrate even our smallest of accomplishments. This self-encouragement propels us to our goal.

Cherish the progress that you see.

Your Ego Will Fight You

Your ego has an investment in the status quo, and fears that it will be destroyed by your transformation. Like a child who suddenly has a younger sibling, the ego jealously guards its turf.

Teach your ego a new way. That is why we learned earlier to transform the different parts of the ego.

- When your ego feels threatened, balance its influence by inviting it into your safe inner space, where you can reconnect it with the Source of creativity, power and grace.

- When your inner judge is frightened by a new situation, retrain it to discern the truth in the situation based on a new set of maxims.

- When your inner critic disapproves, teach it to accept your outer circumstances as they are, and redeploy it to help you move forward to where you would like to be by dissecting information and discerning the truth in any situation.

- When your inner saint is afraid that it will be punished for not living up to its standard of perfection, teach it that the current situation does not have to match its impossible, idealized view.

- When your inner sinner feels guilty because of its destructive behavior or overindulgence, instead of suppressing its energy, redeploy it in balanced, productive ways.

- When the inner child reverts to behavior that is unacceptable in an adult world, repeatedly bring it into your safe inner space until it re-connects with the force and the divine purpose and potential of your life and, once unharnessed, astounds you with its wisdom, strength, creativity, vision and power.

As we continually identify the parts of our ego that resist healing, we become increasingly adept at invoking grace to move us forward. When your ego fights you, remember that you don't have to fight back. Instead, turn the other cheek. Fighting only amplifies the resistance, because what you resist persists. Teach your ego a new way, and you will gradually usher it into a new consciousness.

God Has Your Back

As you achieve your good, you become an example for others. Your light becomes a beacon for all who are searching for a way out of their dark places. Without saying a word, you become a way-shower. The energy that you exude touches people and their consciousness just as you smile to a stranger who then smiles to another.

This ripple effect is how consciousness on the earth shifts so we all have a prosperity consciousness. God has an investment in your good, and wants for you what you want for yourself. As long as you believe that God has your back, all will be well.

When you have a moment of doubt, pray for a case of *divine amnesia*. Forget to doubt, judge, or withhold prosperity from yourself and, instead, return to the great moment of the present.

God has your back.

Dance in Advance

In the Bible, King David retrieved the Ark of the Covenant, which symbolized the spark of divinity that lives within each human and was said to bless those who possessed it. As David entered the city with the Ark, he was so excited that he started dancing a dance of joy before taking the Ark to its new location in the tabernacle. King David was willing to dance in advance.

What King David tapped into (pun intended) was the faith, acceptance, and expectation that connects us with the One Power, the One Spirit, the One Source of our prosperity. This connection is truly a reason to be happy, to dance in advance.

Practice Patience

One of the key myths of prosperity is that it happens by grace.

Prosperity happens with practice.

Practice experiencing the grace that draws prosperity to you and draws you to your prosperity. When you experience this state of grace from within, it draws gracious prosperity to you in your outer world. When you continually practice spiritual principles in your everyday life, your inner life becomes more aligned with the highest energy of creation possible, and manifesting your good becomes second nature to you. This takes practice.

I recall an interview of a Hollywood megastar where the interviewer referred to the star as an overnight sensation. The celebrity replied, "I'm an overnight sensation that was twenty years in the making." Just as a duck that paddles steadily under the water appears to be floating gracefully, this entertainer had been practicing his craft, preparing to make it in the business for almost two decades before his big break came. To the outside observer, it seemed like sudden success when, in fact, his success was built on two decades of experience and persistence that finally paid off.

We continually practice our spiritual principles until they become second nature, and our breakthrough occurs. Practice includes attempting to create your good even if you don't succeed in the way that you envisioned. Just as you have to play the lottery to win the lottery, you create your own good as a signal to the universe that you are becoming increasingly ready to accept even more good.

And when you fail, you have not failed. You have received valuable feedback from the universe alerting you to a subconscious obstacle to your good that you have identified and are now ready to heal. Only the ego would call this a failure, because it does not want you to succeed. It wants you to be stuck where you are so that it, and not the higher nature of your true being, can control your life. Like Babe Ruth, you are acquiring valuable data with each strikeout.

Balance Patience and Persistence

Obviously, the patience and persistence necessary to have a joyful journey of prosperity must be in balance. You are out of balance when tasks seem heavy and require effort. You are in balance when tasks seem more effortless. When tasks require effort, you are going against the flow of the universe that is designed to support you. When tasks require less effort, you are in the flow of the universe's creative process.

To stay in the flow, use the meditation practices that were described earlier. These practices open you to the energy of the universe that would flow effortlessly though you, guiding you along the path of least resistance. You can also gain valuable insights that will help you to avoid stumbling blocks. This is why it is important to take the time to meditate.

If you don't have time for meditation, you might not have time to create your greatest prosperity.

First, seek the peace, power, creative energy, wisdom, guidance, expectancy and joy that come with meditation, and all else happens more effortlessly, and joyfully. To repeat myself once again, this is an outgrowth of the scripture, "Seek ye first the kingdom of God" (which is heaven, and lies within you) "and all these things shall be added unto you."

Balance Pragmatism and Idealism

Do the inner work of prosperity. Also, work in the outer world to manifest prosperity. Don't try to win the lottery without going to your neighborhood 7-11 to buy a ticket. Faith without work is futile.

Work without faith wastes energy, because faith pulls you forward toward your prosperity.

Pause to Refuel

The path to prosperity is not a drag race. In longer races, a driver who is low on fuel makes pit stops because he has a long-term view and is not worried about losing a few seconds. He knows that to complete the race, he must refuel, check vital indicators and restart.

This is the viewpoint that you must acquire when developing and manifesting our prosperity. Do not judge your pit stops. They refuel your spiritual journey. And do not judge yourself for needing them. These pit stops are a necessary part of the rhythm of creation which, just like the tides, has a natural ebb and flow.

In our male-dominated consciousness, which values *doing* over *being*, we often experience an intensity that thwarts your prosperity when we fail to make a pit stop. This intensity is indicative of an underlying fear. We may believe that we are simply intent on creating what we want, but this intensity is laced with anxiety borne of lack. If our core energy is lack, we magnify lack instead of the desire that we are creating, and the lack perpetuates itself.

Be vigilant of any intensity that can thwart our creation. Without proper pacing, you may tire and quit right before the blessing appears. Hollywood is littered with successful actors whose big break came in the form of a phone call that happened just as they were leaving their apartments with their bags packed for their return trip to Kansas.

Find Your Label

The biggest obstacle that stands between most people and prosperity is the subconscious idea that we do not deserve our good because of a label. When we focus on our left-handedness, our unworthiness, or even on a label that we believe defines us— our race, social status, financial status, physical size or appearance, sexual orientation, etc.—we deny ourselves the transcendent power of our unlimited and unlabeled spiritual essence, and we limit our experience. Like the elephant tied to a small stake early in life, we do not believe that we can simply walk away, not from who we are, but from any fear, shame, self-doubt, anger, or obstacle that limits us.

Your only label is Beloved.

Enjoy the Ride

God wants for you what you want for yourself. God is not a force designed to thwart your desires. God is the force that helps you create and manifest your desires. Any resistance to creating your good is due to guilt, lack of clarity, or creations that are not aligned with unconditional love.

As you continue to work with your prosperity, your desires naturally move more into alignment with unconditional love. Your vision becomes clearer when it is more fully fused with God's vision for you. Your resistance to your good fades as God's grace heals old wounds and inner conflicts.

When you order at a restaurant, you order. You simply state your desire to the server, who instructs the kitchen staff to fulfill your desire. You don't beg, you don't plead, and you don't whine. Once you have ordered, you continue to enjoy your dining partners as the different courses of the meal are brought to you. You don't worry about the noise or heat of the kitchen because you know that good food is coming.

When you place your order to the universe, God is the chef. You are the client. Angels are the servers. It is God's pleasure to pour you out a blessing, for God's intention is for His joy, creativity and experience to be magnified through you, His creation.

So, have fun with your creative process. Treat the inner work as a big game. Enjoy every mile of the journey, even those miles that your ego judges as wrong turns, for they have valuable lessons to teach you. Find joy in your incremental healing, and in your big and small victories.

Enjoy the ride!

A Not-So-Final Word

I hope you will return to this book again and again, read and reread the parts that speak to you, and repeat the exercises as you continue along your way to the prosperity that you have chosen. When you encounter an obstacle, or take a wrong turn:

> *Rinse and repeat.*

Acknowledgements

First of all, I'd like to express my gratitude to the universe for supporting me in the completion of this project. It has been in the making for years, and the universe eventually sent the perfect support to me in the form of people and life circumstances necessary in order for me to complete it.

Thanks to Carl Poleskey's constant support and Daniel Neusom's constant counsel, I was able to stay true to my dream of offering the gift of these understandings to others.

Thanks to the members and friends of my spiritual community, the Takoma Metaphysical Chapel, whose support and encouragement buoyed me and confirmed that the wisdom contained in this book could be of help to others.

Thanks to my editors, Jenetha McCutcheon Hollis, and David Parrish, author of *Losing Jon,* who helped me to de-construct and re-construct this book in a way that will be useful to so many.

Finally, thanks to the friends *who* patiently understood while I had my nose *buried in this book.*